D1104309

THE

PLAYS AND POEMS

OF

CYRIL TOURNEUR.

THE

PLAYS AND POEMS

OF

CYRIL TOURNEUR

EDITED

𝔚𝔦𝔱𝔥 𝔆𝔯𝔦𝔱𝔦𝔠𝔞𝔩 𝔍𝔫𝔱𝔯𝔬𝔡𝔲𝔠𝔱𝔦𝔬𝔫 𝔞𝔫𝔡 𝔑𝔬𝔱𝔢𝔰

By JOHN CHURTON COLLINS

IN TWO VOLUMES.—VOL. I.

BOOKS FOR LIBRARIES PRESS

FREEPORT, NEW YORK

First Published 1878
Reprinted 1972

INTERNATIONAL STANDARD BOOK NUMBER:
0-8369-6787-9

LIBRARY OF CONGRESS CATALOG CARD NUMBER:
77-38370

PRINTED IN THE UNITED STATES OF AMERICA
BY
NEW WORLD BOOK MANUFACTURING CO., INC.
HALLANDALE, FLORIDA 33009

TO

ALGERNON CHARLES SWINBURNE

THESE VOLUMES

𝔄𝔯𝔢 𝔍𝔫𝔰𝔠𝔯𝔦𝔟𝔢𝔡

WITH

RESPECT AND AFFECTION.

PREFACE.

HE delay in bringing out these volumes has arisen from my anxiety to discover something of the particulars of Tourneur's life, but I am sorry to say I have not been successful; and his biography is likely to remain a blank, unless some future explorer should be more fortunate than myself.

In settling the text I have been careful to eschew conjecture, and to adhere closely to the quartos. This has been very necessary in the case of the *Revenger's Tragedy*, (the only one of these works which has been edited before,) as the editors have often rashly and un‧ necessarily tampered with the text, even where it was quite intelligible and definite. The text of the *Atheist's Tragedy* I have been obliged in a great measure to recast, and have restored the blank verse, much of which had been printed as prose. I have not altered, however, more than half a dozen words in the whole play—which are scrupulously noted. With regard to the *Transformed Metamorphosis*, I can only say I have done my best to throw light upon the excessive obscurity which perplexes it, though I am far from asserting that a plausible interpretation is necessarily the right one. For the orthography, I have thought it well to keep as close as possible to the original, with the exception of modernising certain spellings which might unnecessarily offend the eye of the reader. U, for instance, has usually been altered into V, and the apostrophic comma has been inserted. The punctuation has of course been revised throughout.

I have to express my thanks to Mr. Samuel Gardiner for one or two valuable suggestions, and for going through the whole of the *Transformed Metamorphosis*. To Mr. Payne Collier I am obliged for his helping me to trace a pamphlet which I once thought was to be attributed to Tourneur. To the courtesy of Sir Charles Isham I owe the use of the *Transformed Metamorphosis*, and to its discoverer, Mr. Charles Edmonds, I am also indebted, not only for his generosity in waiving his own claims to reprinting this poem, that my work might be enriched by it, but for the ready kindness with which he has always assisted me with his great bibliographical experience. To the Rev. A. B. Grosart I am very much obliged for some ingenious suggestions touching the interpretation of the *Transformed Metamorphosis*, though I am sorry I have not been able to avail myself of more than one or two of them.

In conclusion, I beg to thank the assistant librarians of the British Museum for the courtesy and readiness—more than official—with which they have responded to the many calls I have been obliged to make on their time and attention.

J. CHURTON COLLINS.

5, *King's Bench Walk, Temple.*

INTRODUCTION.

HAT Shakespeare was but the sun of a mighty system, and had necessarily eclipsed in his meridian splendour the glories of his satellites, was idly conjectured by the acutest critic of the eighteenth century, and has been exactly verified by the conscientious industry of our own. The unerring taste and nice discernment of Lamb, the searching and comprehensive criticism of Coleridge, the impetuous enthusiasm and analytical subtlety of Hazlitt, were fortunately directed to the noble task of remembering their forgotten countrymen, of recognising and resuscitating buried merit, and of doing justice where justice had been so long and so shamefully deferred. When such illustrious leaders undertake and consecrate a cause, they are not likely to want followers ; though it too often

happens that the follower succeeds to the cheap
heritage of the enthusiasm without succeeding to
any share in the discernment of his masters. The
keen and cultured discrimination of a Lamb can
sift the treasure it discovers ; but to the omnivorous
voracity of the Dibdens and Shakespeare Societies
indirectly called into being by him, all is equally
acceptable and all equally valuable. Criticism
dies, and Bibliography, its bastard child, is born :
fruitful investigation ends, and a barren mania
begins.

During the last fifty years no department of our
literature has been so exhaustively and inde-
fatigably studied as the Elizabethan drama. Its very
refuse and rinsings have been hailed with a superstitious reverence ridiculous in its excess and grotesque in its expression. There is scarcely a name
among the innumerable dramatists who thronged the
English stage from 1562 to 1640, which is not now
more familiar to a large body of modern students
than any of the masters of the eighteenth century
or any of the poets of the present. It would be
difficult to name a single play out of the hundreds
of plays good, bad, and indifferent thrown off in
the careless prodigality of those prolific pens, which
has not now found its reader, its critic, and its
panegyrist.

Not only has the really peerless work of Marlowe, Webster, and Ford ; the interesting and excellent work of Dekker, Heywood, Middleton, and Chapman ; the respectable work of Greene, Peele, Lyly, Marston, and Shirley, found the ample recognition which was its due, but so completely has the task of collecting, annotating, and commenting been performed, that by the mere process of exhaustion we may presume, an enterprising publisher has arrived at Henry Glapthorne ; and doubtless before long, Goff, Field, Nabbes, and Gomersal will appear with all their blushing honours thick upon them. One great name has, however, been forgotten : one dark and sullen figure has been passed unnoticed by the prying glance of modern connoisseurs, as he passed unnoticed in the careless indifference of his contemporaries.

The author of the " Revenger's Tragedy," a play in sustained intensity of tragic grandeur second only to the masterpieces of Shakespeare and Webster — of the " Atheist's Tragedy," a work which, in easy sweetness of style, mellow and mellifluous versification, wealth of exquisite imagery, and happy expression, is the mete mate of Shakespeare's earlier romances, — a great poet, who has stamped deep on every page he has written the expression of a powerful, anomalous, unique genius, has as yet found no editor ; while his works have been left to moulder away in seventeenth century quartos, or to jostle their inferiors, mauled and mangled in execrable reprints. Though the grave Muse of Bibliography has her caprices, and does not always see as her sisters see, it is difficult to account for her neglect of these works, especially as they have long been introduced to her notice by men whom she usually respects. Lamb in a memorable passage has recognised Tourneur's supreme tragic excellence. Hazlitt has spoken of his " dazzling fence of impassioned argument," his " pregnant illustration," and his " profound reaches of thought which lay open the soul of feeling." The writer of an article in the *Retrospective Review,* so far back as 1823, has given emphatic testimony to his extraordinary merit, and amply supported the eulogy by long extracts ; another, writing in the *New Monthly Magazine,* has performed ably and eloquently the same service. Mr. Swinburne, seven years ago, graphically characterised the " unquenchable and burning fire, the bitter ardour and angry beauty of his verse," and his " keenness and mastery of passionate expression." Nor are these his only claim to our interest and consideration. His influence is distinctly traceable in the writings of the so-called " spasmodic school" of the present century. His terse and telling phrases have been pillaged; his trick of pungent and powerful epigrammatical expression has been caught and copied, his original and striking images have been appropriated without any acknowledgment, and the dangerous freak played by Warburton with Milton's prose works, and by Rowe with Massinger's dramas, has been repeated with the same motive and on the same principle with the " Atheist's Tragedy " and the " Revenger's Tragedy."

Cyril Tourneur, Tournour, or Turner, for he spells his name in the three ways, was a poet who flourished in the latter end of Elizabeth's reign and the beginning of James I. His life is wrapped in impenetrable obscurity. Where and when he was born, where and when he died, it seems impossible to ascertain. That he had written nothing of any consequence before 1600 is pretty certain from the fact that nothing of his is quoted in " England's Parnassus ;" that he was engaged in poetical composition between 1600 and 1613 we gather from the dates of his various works, and that he was employed as a professional writer we learn from the Alleyn Papers, in a letter dated June 5, 1613, addressed by Robert Daborne, a well-known playwright, to Philip Henslowe :

"Mr. Hinchlow, the Company told me y^u wear expected thear yesterday to conclude about there coming over or going to Oxford I have not only labord to my own play which shall be ready before they come over but given Cyrill Tourneur an act of ye arreignment of London to write y^t we may have y^t likewise ready for them."

Winstanley quotes a couplet by some anonymous author which implies that he was not much known or noticed by his contemporaries :

"His fame unto that pitch so only rais'd
As not to be despis'd nor too much prais'd."

And as there is no mention of him, so far as I can discover, in Henslowe's "Diary," the presumption is that his dealings with managers were not very extensive ; though this negative evidence will not go for much, as he may have been connected with some of the other theatres. If Taylor in his "Praise of Hempseed," Heywood in his "Hierarchie of the Blessed Angels," and the authors of "Wits' Recreations" had not maintained an obstinate silence about him when he was certainly alive, we might conclude that he was dead in 1615, as Edmund Hawes, in his "Continuation of Stowe's Annals," giving an elaborate list of the poets then living, omits to mention him. His minute acquaintance with legal technicalities would lead us to suspect that he might have been connected in some way with the profession of the law. But the sleepless energy of the Renaissance, and the necessity for realistic appeals to their various, practical, and demonstrative audience led most of the Elizabethan dramatists to familiarise themselves with the technicalities of almost every trade and profession; and in this department of troublesome and conscientious labour they need fear no comparison even with Honoré de Balzac and—one blushes to have to unite such discordant names —Mr. Charles Reade. An allusion, however, to the " eight returns " of Michaelmas Term, in the " Revenger's Tragedy"—a piece of minute information, which as a mere outsider he would have been scarcely likely to possess, makes it not unlikely that he was a member of one of the Inns of Court, like so many of his brother dramatists — Norton, Wilmot, Lodge, Beaumont, Ford, and others. But I have sought in vain for any traces of him. This absence of all biographical detail is, in the present case, singularly unfortunate ; for the reader of these works cannot fail to feel that a character of no common interest, must have thus passed without any record away—

a career of no common vicissitudes have vanished with its vanished actor.

If we are in possession of a complete list of Tourneur's writings, which I venture to think is improbable, his first acknowledged publication was the "Transformed Metamorphosis." This appeared in 1600, printed by the well-known publisher, Valentine Sims, and dedicated, in terms of the usual hyperbolic pedantry, to Sir Christopher Heydon, a man who had fought for his country successfully as a soldier, and was now fighting for folly unsuccessfully as an astrologer. The history of this extraordinary work, which was, as its author informs us, written at leisure moments in three weeks, is not a little curious. It is a neat duodecimo volume, faultlessly printed and punctuated in a neat, clear type, with an illustrated title-page. Till the year 1872, when it was accidentally discovered by Mr. Charles Edmonds at Lamport Hall, in Hampshire, its very existence was unknown and even unsuspected, for there is no record of it on the stationers' books or in any known catalogue. There is apparently an allusion to it in Taylor's "Mad Fashions, Odd Fashions, All out of Fashions, or The Emblems of These Distracted Times:"

> " For if you well do note it as it is,
> It is a *Transformed Metamorphosis ;*
> This monstrous picture plainly doth declare
> This land quite out of order," etc.

But that is the only one I can discover. No other copy or fragment of this work has been noticed by bibliographers, and if the gentleman who unearthed it has not succeeded in presenting English literature with a Tzetzes, he may at least congratulate himself that he has presented it with a Lycophron. The " Cassandra" and the " Transformed Metamorphosis" have certainly little enough in common, though the one is probably quite as much worth unravelling as the other, if the shades of Charles Fox and Gilbert Wakefield will forgive the remark. Tourneur's poem, without a running commentary, is not only obscure, but utterly and hopelessly unintelligible ; every line is a *crux*, every stanza an enigma, requiring not an Œdipus but a Lynceus. The author informs us that it was written in three weeks during leisure hours, and that it is a satire; but that as he wishes to avoid personalities, he simply speaks generally, or, in other words, he lashes vices, but spares particular allusions. Its excessive obscurity arises as much from the abnormal and grotesque mould in which the whole poem is cast, as from the hideous jargon in which it is written.

b—2

It is possible that its author may have been compelled for several reasons to write in this enigmatical language, more especially as he was dealing with political questions of some nicety, and expressing sympathy with a patron who had already been concerned in rebellion, and was probably trembling for his life.*

If, however, we view the poem in connection with the satirical literature which immediately preceded it, we shall find that after all it is only one of a kindred group. The prologue, for instance, of Middleton's "Microcynicon," which appeared in 1599, resembles very closely the commencement of Tourneur's work. They both employ the same extravagant imagery to express the same simple idea. Tourneur pictures himself as seeking and finding a steadfast rock, surrounded on one side with a raging sea, on the other with flames, that he may see and satirise the tragic scenes around him. Middleton imagines himself in a similar position :

> "Environed with a brazen tower,
> I little dread their stormy, raging power,
> Witnessing this black defying embassie;"

and then proceeds to depict similar vices to those depicted by Tourneur.

As for the style of Tourneur's work, it is merely

* See Blomefield's "History of Norfolk," vol. vi., p. 507.

the exaggerated form of a style—and this is important—which had lately become fashionable. A
school of writers had arisen, with Hall and Marston
at their head, whose principal ambition would seem
to have been to stand in the same relation to
classical English as Callimachus and Lycophron
stand to classical Greek, and as Persius stands to
classical Latin ; to corrupt, that is to say, their
native language and to create a detestable language of their own. This they managed to do
by substituting for simple words hideous sesqui-
pedalian compounds coined indiscriminately from
Latin and Greek ; by affecting the harshest classical
phraseology and constructions; by loading their
pages with obscure mythological allusions; by the
systematic employment and abuse of ellipse ; by
adopting technical expressions borrowed sometimes
from astrology, at other times from alchymy, and
occasionally also from theology, casuistry, and scho-
lasticism ; and by torturing language and thought
into every kind of fantastic absurdity. The finest
and completest specimen of the writings of this
school the reader will now for the first time have
an opportunity of inspecting in " The Transformed
Metamorphosis ;" though even Tourneur must have
viewed with a sort of admiring despair the genius
which could produce such gems as "rough-hewn
teretismes," "logogryphs," "acholithite," "semele-

femorigena," "mastigophoros eyne," "vizarded-
bifronted-Janian," "aphrogenias, ill-yoked," "the
ophiogine of Hellespont," "mistagogus," "ena-
gonian," "collybist,"* etc. He must have felt
indeed at times uncomfortably aware that the
clouds which enfold what meaning he may happen
to possess, were but as twilight to the genuine night
of Hall and Marston. The style of these writers
has been graphically characterised by the latter
one of its greatest masters,—and as his words
exactly describe Tourneur's poem as well as Hall's,
I shall quote the passage at length :

> " Our modern satyr's sharpest lines
> Whose hungry fangs snarle at some secret sin.
> And in such pitchie clouds enwrapped been
> His Sphinxian riddles, that old Œdipus
> Would be amaz'd and take it in foul snufs
> That such Cymerian darkness should involve
> A quaint conceit that he could not resolve.
> O darknes palpable ! Egipt's black night !
> My wit is stricken blind, hath lost his sight ;
> My shins are broke with groping for some sense
> To know to what his words have reference.
>
> *   *   *   *   *
>
> Delphic Apollo, ayde me to unrip
> These intricate deepe oracles of wit,
> These dark enigmas and strange riddling sense ;
> Fie on my senceless pate !"

The sudden outburst of satire during the last ten

---

* These barbarisms have been culled indiscriminately from the
satires of Hall and Marston, and are very far from exhausting the
list.

years of the sixteenth century is in itself interesting and remarkable; but that these satirists should
have agreed to express themselves in a jargon like
this—for not even Lodge is altogether free from it
—is inexplicable. It is not impossible that they
imagined themselves imitating Persius, who has
always been a favourite with the English satirists ;
though it is singular that while adopting it themselves, they never failed with the ludicrous incon-
sistency of their master to ridicule it in others. The
passage just quoted is Marston's sarcastic description
of his adversary Hall's diction, though it applies with
literal and exquisite felicity to his own. That the
vices of the age, as well as the vocabulary of its
poets, afforded fair subjects and ample scope for
satire, is probable enough ; and both Marston and
Tourneur have emphatically described the agonies
of shame and grief with which the daily contemplation of triumphant iniquity and a licentious style
had racked them. But what appears especially to
have grated on their chaste and pious ears, which
were probably the chastest part about them, was the
licentious tone of much of the current poetical literature. Marlowe's translation of Ovid's "Amores,"
Shakespeare's "Venus and Adonis," Cutwode's
"Caltha Poetarum," the epigrams of Davies and
Harrington, a singularly gross version of the "Ars

Amatoria," the coarse and often indecent verses and
pamphlets written by Greene and Nash, had tried
severely the morality or the prudery of the nation,
and called loudly for satirical castigation, no doubt;
but to find the author of " Pigmalion's Image" and
the delineator of Levidulcia and Snuffe among the
prophets, is certainly startling and not quite satis-
factory.   Tourneur had evidently studied atten-
tively Marston's two poems, modelling to some
extent his style on them, and closely imitating their
general tone.   That he was a young man when he
produced his amorphous and barbarous work may
rather be assumed from the fact of his choosing
Marston as a model, than from any internal evidence derived from crudities of style and thought,
for to these peculiarities he clung doggedly to the
last, as the "Grief on Prince Henry" abundantly
testifies.

We have now to deal with one of those singular
errors which sometimes creep into bibliography,
and are not a little confusing—in the present case
not a little disappointing too. In 1605 appeared a
small quarto in black letter, entitled "Laugh and
Lie Down"—["Laugh and Lie Down: or the World's
Folly   Printed at London for Jeffrey Chorlton
and are to be sold at his shop at the great North
dore of Saint Paules 1605   4to"]. This has been

alluded to more than once, as a comedy. It is really a short tract written in prose, and appears to be an allegory* describing the Fort of Folly and the persons who inhabited it. Interspersed with the narrative we find fifteen popular ballads, (among them, " Come, live with me," etc., variations of " Three merry men be we," " All the Green Willow," etc.,) some of which, as Mr. Collier says, importantly illustrate Shakespeare, and there its literary interest ends. But following the title-page is a brief address " To the Reader," with a dedication " To his most loved, loving and wel beloved no matter whom C. T." Now, we have no means whatever of determining to whom these initials belong save on purely conjectural grounds; but the tract falling into the hands of Isaac Reed, he assigned them, tentatively, we must presume, to Cyril Tourneur. What with Reed was simple conjecture, hardened with others into established fact, and the tract was accordingly entered on the catalogue at his sale in 1807 as Cyril Tourneur's; it has been enrolled by Lowndes among the acknowledged works of Tourneur, and confidently assigned to him ever since. There is, however, no reason at all for believing him to be the author. There is, in the first place, no internal evidence to support such a

---

* Collier; see the article in his " Bibliographical Account."

supposition; on the contrary, there is much to overthrow it.*

The cynical quaintness of the dedication, which may have had its weight in inducing Reed to assign it to Tourneur, is certainly in his manner; but it is no distinctive mark, for such epigrams are common enough in the dedications of the time; see, for instance, the dedication to William Goddard's "Mastiff's Whelps," and Marston's "Scourge of Villainy." If it be Tourneur's it is the only work to which he has not signed his name.

C. T. and T. C are anonymous signatures, familiar to the students of Elizabethan pamphlet literature; and if the initials are in this particular case to be assigned to Tourneur, why should we not hold him responsible for other contemporary tracts so signed? Are we to attribute to him, for instance, "A Notable History of Nastagio and Traversari, translated out of Italian into English verse by C. T., 8vo., 1569;" or, "An Advice how to plant tobacco in England, and how to bring it to colour and perfection, by C. T., 1615."? If we are to include any one of these publications in his works, there is nothing but the most arbitrary principle of selec-

---

* The combined effects of drunkenness, starvation, and paralysis could never sink a man of genius in such an abyss of fatuity as the extract admiringly given by Mr. Collier reveals.

tion to prevent us from including all, for they are all equally devoid of internal evidence, equally unimportant, and equally worthless.

In 1609 appeared " The Funeral Poem on the Death of Sir Francis Vere," one of the most distinguished military commanders of the age. Thus entered in the stationers' books :

" Entred for his copie, under Master Waterson's hand and Master Wilson's, a booke called ' A General Poem upon the death of the most worthy Soldyour, Sir Ffrancis Vere, Knight.' Vjd."

This poem is a barren miracle of cold-blooded analytical panegyric, giving a weary catalogue of all the moral and intellectual excellencies possible to man, and then establishing with a mathematical precision—so grotesque that we may shrewdly suspect the cynical poet to be all the while laughing in his sleeve—the fact that Vere possessed them all. It must certainly exhaust the acquirements of any hero and as certainly exhaust the patience of any reader. The least that can be said for it is that, in its vigorous verse, its occasional originality and happy imagery, it is much above the average of such eulogies, and sometimes reminds us of Dryden—at his worst.

His next poem, for I reserve the plays for the present, was the " Grief on the Death of Prince Henry." The event which inspired this work took

place on Friday, Nov. 6th, 1612; and if the English people lost a prince of whom they may have
been proud, English literature gained a mass of
fatuous balderdash of which it ought to be heartily
ashamed.   The unfortunate youth was scarcely
cold in his grave when his country appears to have
broken out into a sort of husky howl.   Some of our
noblest poets suspended their labours to prostitute
their genius by uniting with the scum of their own
profession and with the scum of another not less
ambitious but more impotent, though it had the
advantage of the pulpit, to lay a barren and loathsome tribute on the grave of the amiable boy, that
they might, in thus toadying the memory of a dead
son, toady the patronage of a living parricide.
George Chapman, who had, however, some excuse
for engaging in the degrading business, suspended
the composition of his magnificent declamations
to snuffle out in his worst style a Funeral Elegy on
" the most disastrous death," etc.   Drummond of
Hawthornden, defying "the stars to do their worst,"
hid his unseemly agony in mythology—its appropriate place.   Heywood, who was probably either
starving or in prison, followed; and Webster,
disgraced, and tarnished, for the first and last time,
a noble and manly literary career.   William
Basse informed an indifferent world that its " sun

was sett," and bewailed it in a "shower of tears."
An anonymous author, whose name, however, probably managed to reach the ears of his stricken
sovereign, presented his "sunless country" with a
"Mourning Garment." The lamentations of Cam-
pion, Hall, Brooke, Donne, and Taylor, the water-poet
—the most pestilent driveller that ever glutted the
grocers—were echoed, owl-like, back in Latin by the
two Universities. The reverend Heads, however,
of those illustrious seminaries, unlike some of their
successors in the present day, rarely sought, in an
honourable position, mean occasions for neglecting
its duties to lacquey those with whom their responsible post had brought them into irrelevant contact,
or, if they did so, could plead, like Gibbon, that
they had "veiled their shame in the obscurity of a
learned language," and not paraded it in naked
defiance for all to inspect, loathe, and laugh at.

But England was not alone. Dominic Baudius,
scenting carrion from afar, even from Leyden, where
things were not going well with him, quitted his
officious politics and vagrant amours to construct a
"Monumentum Consecratum," etc., and others
hasted to similarly degrade themselves.

Tourneur's poem was one of a trio published together, in quarto, by William Welbie, in 1613. The
other two, entitled respectively a "Monumental

Columne " and a " Funeral Elegy," were written by
the dramatists, John Webster and Thomas Heywood, the first in heroics, the second in the ottava
rima. The work is entered in the Stationers' books,
December 25th, 1612:

" Master Welby—entred for his copie vnder th[e
h]and of Master Harrison Warden A booke
called funerall Elegies vpon the death of prince
Henry, by Cirill Turnour, John Webster, Thomas
Hayward.   Vjd."

Tourneur's portion of it is dedicated, it will be
seen, to a Master George Carie ; but I regret to
find that, from the very general terms in which he
is addressed, it is quite impossible to identify him
in the crowd of Careys and Carews who were attached to the Court of James I. A careful investigation, however, of some of the State Papers, Somer's
Tracts, the Harleian Miscellany, Cornwallis and
other contemporary documents, enables me to assert
with some confidence that there is no Master
George Carie recorded as holding any office in the
Prince's Court, as Tourneur's language would seem
to imply. We may presume, therefore, that this
particular person had as much reason for honouring
him much and faithfully as his dedicator had for
thanking him for doing so. To express gratitude

to a patron for honouring a prince is one of those graceful but officious conceits which have been indulged in by poets inferior to Tourneur, and succeeded in pleasing courtiers superior to Carey.

Though this "Grief" is happily very short, the writer has managed to condense into it not a little dulness and obscurity, with a more than usual share of his most unpleasant mannerisms—elliptic commonplaces, bald platitudes assuming under mere tricks of style, the appearance of originality, rugged metre, and imperfectly-embodied thoughts. His grief, no doubt, choked his utterance. Though apparently his last performance, it is beyond all question his worst, and is as affected and absurd in style as it is false and puerile in sentiment.

What Petrarch's "Africa" is to his Canzoni and Sonnets, what Spenser's "Shepherd's Calendar" is to his "Faëry Queene," what Milton's "Elegy on Hobson" is to his "Elegy on Edward King," that are Tourneur's poems to his plays—and at his plays we have now arrived. His poems were written obviously to catch patronage and to fill his purse ; his plays are his soul's voice, the authentic expression of his life's work. His poems, with all their varied literary and historical value, are but the hollow and insincere productions of ephemeral art dealing with ephemeral topics : his plays are

the imperishable records of imperishable passions—
the solid and eternal pillars on which rests im-
movably a splendid immortality.

The first in order of chronology, the first, undoubtedly, in order of merit, but the last, I am
convinced, in order of composition, is the "Revenger's Tragedy." This, by the way, has another
title viz.—"The Loyal Brother," given to it in two
or three theatrical lists of the early eighteenth
century, and is assigned inaccurately to T. Turner.
It was entered on the Stationers' books, with a play
of Middleton's, 7th of October, 1607.

"George Elde Entred for his copies vnder th[e
h]andes of Sir George Bucke and th[e] wardens Twoo
plaies th[e] one called the revenger's tragedie th[e]
other A trick to catch the old one. xijd."

There are two quartos, one of 1607, and one of
1608 : these are not the same edition with different
title-pages, as has been alleged, though the mistake
was a natural one, and nothing but a careful colla-
tion would have been likely to detect it. The variations in the text of these quartos,* which do not
amount to more than three or four, occur towards the
end of the play : for the rest, they remain, with all

* Two are important, viz : "Nake your swords," 1608, for
"Make"; and in scene iv. act iv., "We will make *you* blush," is
altered by second edition into "yron."

their errors, the same.   The quartos form no exception to the rule, but are full of inaccuracies and
confusion : the exits and entrances are very imperfectly noted, and in both editions there is no fifth
act marked ; but the actual text is tolerably correct
—as a rule correctly punctuated, and carefully dis-
criminating verse from prose, thus making it not improbable that the proofs were revised by the author
—a rare circumstance in those days.   He must certainly have inserted the two striking alterations
which appear in the later quarto.

Whether Tourneur got his plot from any Italian
or French novel I am unable, after much troublesome investigation, to say : it is, however, so subtly
complicated and so dramatically suitable that it
probably came, like Ford's kindred atrocities, "out
of the carver's brain ;" and the allegorical nomenclature adopted for the dramatis personæ would
seem to point to the same conclusion.   This play
has been thrice reprinted : once by Dodsley, once
in another old collection, and again the other day,
under the supervision of Mr. Carew Hazlitt—I am
sorry to say not very carefully, and with a licence
of conjectural emendation often aggravating and
generally unnecessary.

"'The Atheist's Tragedy ; or, the Honest Man's
Revenge,' as in divers places it has often been

acted," was first printed in 1611. Thus on the Stationers' books:

"September 11th John Stepneth Entred for his copye vnder th[e h]andes of Sir George Bucke and Th[e] Wardens a booke called the Tragedy of the Atheist."

This is the only edition, though Reed and Baker, in the "Biographia Dramatica," give 1612 as the date of the play, which made me think there may have been a second edition. I can, however, find no trace of it. This tragi-comedy, for such it obviously aims at being, has never, for some inexplicable reason, been included in any collection, and has only been once reprinted; that was in 1792, an execrable production, which to all the blunders of the quarto adds still more atrocious blunders of its own. The text of the quarto is in a deplorable state—verse and prose are jumbled indiscriminately together, the punctuation is ludicrously incorrect, all is in confusion. The plot, or rather the series of melodramatic incidents which usurps its name, is obviously original, though it is possible that the germ of it may be lurking somewhere in contemporary French records, to which Chapman had recently directed attention. A cursory glance through Thuanus, Mezerai, and Jean de Serres has, however, led to nothing.

Beside these two plays, Tourneur was also the author of a third—a tragi-comedy, entitled "The Nobleman," which was never printed. The MS. was in the possession of Warburton, the Somerset Herald, as late as 1815, and was destroyed with many other Elizabethan dramas by his servant* in the course of that year. No account of the style or the subject, of the merits or demerits of the work, has been recorded. It was entered on the Stationers' books, February 15th, 1612, by Edward Blunte:

"Entred for his copy vnder th[e h]andes of Sir George Buc[ke] and the wardens a play booke beinge a Trage comedye called the Nobleman written by Cyrill Tourneur.   vjd."

And from a MS. note of Oldys we learn that it was acted at Court in 1613.

In reviewing Tourneur's dramatic work as a whole, we are confronted at the outset by a problem which it is by no means easy to solve. It must be obvious to every one that these two plays represent two distinct phases in the development of his art; it must be obvious to every one that the earliest of these two phases is represented by the " Atheist's Tragedy," which is the work of a young and inex-

* For a full and complete list of the priceless treasures destroyed by that accursed menial, see *Gentleman's Magazine*, vol. lxxxv., part 2, page 117.

perienced artist ; that the later phase is represented
by the "Revenger's Tragedy," which is plainly the
work of a practised and experienced hand. There
is, indeed, as much difference between the conception and the execution of these two plays as there
is between Shakespeare's work in his first period
and Shakespeare's work in his third period. The
plot of the "Atheist's Tragedy"—and the plot is
usually the weakest point with a young author—is
disconnected, outrageous, and improbable ; the
action is systematically interrupted by irrelevant
episode : the catastrophe is melodramatic and
absurd. The scene is evidently laid in France,
though it is all along confused with English manner and character, a fault shared no doubt by most
of his contemporaries, though they would scarcely
have outraged propriety so far as to introduce such
a person as Snuffe in a French family. The second
and third appearances of Montferrers' silly old
ghost is puerile in the extreme. In the delineation
of the characters, there is a tendency to simple
caricature, and this is sometimes pushed to a grotesque extreme. The conception of the hero is
obviously the ambitious and far-fetched attempt of
a youth to paint what he could not in the nature of
things either realise or understand. Levidulcia is
an imaginative boy's ideal of a Messalina, stolen
doubtless from Marston's Isabella in the "Insatiate

Countess." Marston, however, was no "raw recruit in Aphrodite's host;" and if Joanna of Naples had sat for the general portrait of his infamous heroine, a prudent and artistic economy had no doubt induced him to select living models for the details. False to art, he was perhaps true to nature. His fervid disciple is false to both.

The versification, however, of Tourneur's play is flowing, rich, soft and buoyant ; the lovers—Charlamont and Castabella—are, with all their faults, charmingly portrayed ; and the beauty of isolated passages, embodying sentiments young genius delights in and seldom fails to describe with success, will almost bear comparison even with Shakespeare's work. The whole piece is undoubtedly the production of a young man. Its peculiar defects, its peculiar merits, are the defects and merits peculiar to youth.

If we turn now to the " Revenger's Tragedy," we see at a glance that no youth's hand is here. Everywhere condensed energy, stern, terse, biting phrase ; plot, rough and unhewn no doubt, but imposing, effective, and complete ; principal characters carefully discriminated, consistent, real ; reticence and power ; the consummate work of consummate genius—the crown and flower of long labour, practice, and experience. The date of the publication of these plays is, of course, no criterion of the date of their composition, or even of their appearance

on the stage. We learn, indeed, from Heywood*
that the managers did all they could to prevent
plays being printed ; and this is scarcely to be
wondered at, for the publication of a play was
tantamount to their losing the copyright, for which
they had often paid a high price. Now, I am convinced that the " Atheist's Tragedy," instead of succeeding, preceded the "Revenger's Tragedy;" and I
feel that this must be self-evident to every reader who
has the slightest pretension to any critical insight.
Mere inequality in relative merit goes of course for
nothing—the one may have been a hurried, the
other an elaborate work ; but the immaturity of the
" Atheist's Tragedy" is of such a kind as would
have been impossible in a man who had produced
the " Revenger's Tragedy." There is as much
difference between the crudities and imperfections
of an experienced and an inexperienced artist as
there is between the bad handwriting of a school-
boy and the bad handwriting of an old man. Allow-
ing, however, that the "Atheist's Tragedy" was
written before the "Revenger's," it remains to ex-
plain how its author could spring with one bound
from such comparatively raw and juvenile work, as
we find in the first play, to such firm and effective
work as we find in the second. Such an effort is

* See his interesting address to the reader, prefixed to the "English Traveller."

without parallel in the history of dramatic art, and is quite unintelligible, except on the theory that he produced much more of which we have no record. This is indeed very probable. During the last five years mere accident has unearthed a long printed poem by him, of which, as we have seen, there was no trace at all. We are ignorant of the titles of two-thirds of the two hundred and twenty dramas in which Heywood had a main hand. Of the thirty-eight plays in which we know Chettle was concerned, between 1597 and 1603, four only were printed and have come down to us. It would seem that Daborne was engaged in plays of which no vestige remains; the titles of five have been preserved by a mere chance, and there our knowledge of them ends. There are two plays of Taylor, the Water Poet, mentioned only in one catalogue. And what applies to these four will apply almost without exception to their illustrious contemporaries. The theatrical records of that time are scanty and imperfect. It is more than probable, therefore, that we are in possession of but a small portion of Tourneur's work, and that our losses in the large mass of dramatic literature which was produced on the stage in the golden decade of the drama, and never afterwards printed, has been much more considerable than is usually suspected. The non-completion or disappearance of Heywood's "Lives" has robbed the world of a golden volume which it could ill spare, and must always miss, though it would doubtless have revealed losses of which we are now happily ignorant.

It would be needless to enter at length into an examination of the various attributes which constitute the commanding splendour of Tourneur's genius, for, unlike the coy and retiring merits of subtler artists, they lie in startling prominence on the surface ; but it may be well to notice one or two interesting and distinctive features. He belonged to the school of Shakespeare. The "Atheist's Tragedy" is in its most pleasing and successful passages a study of the master's earlier style. In some cases he has modelled a whole speech with exquisite felicity, on his original, as in Castabella's appeal to D'Amville, in the fourth scene of the third act ; sometimes he copies literal expressions, as in Castabella's prayer at Charlamont's tomb, in the first scene of the same act ; at other times he clothes, in his own words, borrowed scenes and positions, as in the third scene of the fourth act, which is evidently a reminiscence of the churchyard scene in " Hamlet." So subtly and exactly has he caught the ring, phrase, and trick of Shakespeare's style that it would sometimes be impossible to distinguish master from pupil. I would instance among many others :

"To guide your green improvidence of youth
And make you ripe for your inheritance."
                                        Act iii. sc. iv.

"I'll be an instrument
To grace performance with dexteritie."
                                        Act i. sc. ii.

" Be not displeas'd if on
The altar of his tomb I sacrifice
My teares.   They are the jewels of my love
Dissolved into grief, and fall upon
His blasted Spring as April dew upon
A sweet young blossom shak'd before the time."
                                        Act iii. sc. i.

" I am an emperor of a world,
This little world of man.   My passions are
My subjects."   Act iii. sc. iii.

In the " Revenger's Tragedy" he catches much
of his master's later form ; he echoes often his terse
and weighty phrase ; he has borrowed epithets and
touches ; he has selected passages for parodying ; he
has taken types for characters—the younger brother,
for instance, is a close copy of Claudio in " Measure
for Measure,"as Vindici is possibly modelled on Hamlet—but there all resemblance ceases.   At the point
at which most imitators begin, he breaks off to tread
his own lonely and independent path.   To institute
comparisons between inferior men who differ in
degree only, but not in kind, is the legitimate exercise of perverted and harmless ingenuity ; but to
institute comparisons between men of original and
distinctive features is always futile and usually

misleading. Tourneur has been compared to Webster, as the "Revenger's Tragedy" has been compared to Hamlet, and the comparison, as usual, lies
merely on the surface. He has, indeed, none of
those elements in his genius which won for Webster Charles Hazlitt's and Lamb's appropriate and
happy appellation of "the noble-minded ;" he has
none of Webster's breadth and insight, none of his
instinctive sympathy with the great and the true,
none of his searching, subtle pathos, none of that
quick analogical instinct which loads "Vittoria
Corombona" and the "Duchess of Malfi" with
wide-ranging imagery, metaphor, and simile.
Webster has humour, like that of Thucydides—
a humour subdued and severe, peculiar and difficult
to characterise, but seldom altogether absent.
Tourneur has none, for what usurps its name is
either a mocking irony, or, still more frequently, the
gross and quaint expression of some foul passion
stinging within. They were both cynics, but Webster's was the cynicism of a profoundly reflective
intellect, the world-weariness and bitter impatience
which comes upon a great, fearless, sensitive thinker
who sees and feels all, but who cannot always inter-
pret and who will not compromise. If Tourneur is
to be compared with any of his contemporaries he
may be compared appropriately with Marston, but

the parallel, so far as it goes, is so obvious that it is not worth drawing.

Like Juvenal and Marston, he loves to satirise that he may secure for himself the luxury of prurient description. He did not hate men because he hated vice, but he hated vice because he hated men. It is very evident that he had received a classical training and possessed a knowledge probably of the Greek—certainly of the Latin—poets of such a kind that it is not likely to have been second-hand. This accomplishment he occasionally displays, like too many of his contemporaries, with unpleasant ostentation, though at other times it is employed with that apt felicity and unconscious readiness which can only be the result of assimilative thoroughness.

I am certainly inclined to suspect that he had some acquaintance with the Greek tragedians. That his purely sensual conception of the passion of love, however, in which he stands in unenviable solitude among his fellow-dramatists, does not arise from any Hellenic bias, but springs purely from his own diseased and perverted consciousness, cannot, of course, be seriously doubted. It has, it is easy to see, narrowed and damaged his work.

It could hardly be expected, perhaps, that a poet whose instincts lie so entirely on the side of tragedy could possess any comic power, or aim at any comic

effects.   He has, however, unfortunately thought it
necessary to do so, and appears, like Dryden, to
have made a point of substituting indecency for
wit, and mere filth for drollery.   Apollo and Mel-
pomene may have smiled on his tragic offspring,
but his comedy is certainly the joint and vigorous
progeny of Priapus and Cloacina.   His attempts
in this walk, indeed, are at their best only less
contemptible than Marlowe and only less grotesque
than Æschylus, though it must be confessed that
the scene in the churchyard between Snuffe and
Soquette in the "Atheist's Tragedy" will wring out
a reluctant smile hardly to be extorted by the
dreary ribaldry of Wagner in " Doctor Faustus," or
the nauseous babble of the nurse in the " Chöe-
phorœ."   But the Muse of Tragedy has, after all,
been a jealous goddess in the case of all her
votaries save Shakespeare and Racine.   The stage
has seen two, and two only, who could unite the
various and dissimilar powers necessary for the production of an " Othello " and a " Much Ado about
Nothing," of an " Athalie" and a " Les Plaideurs."

To review briefly Tourneur's comic characters.
Dandolo, who appears for a moment in the " Revenger's Tragedy," is a despicable and blundering
parody of Shakespeare's worst farce.   Soquette,
Fresco, etc., in the "Atheist's Tragedy," are below
contempt.   Cataplasma would be intolerable even

in the haunts over which she presides, and Sebastian's wit is as stale as his paramour's love. Languebeau Snuffe is his only attempt of any merit in this walk, but he is at best a vulgar caricature superfluously elaborated and impertinently introduced, a concession, doubtless, to the groundlings, who had, however, been taught to laugh at better things. But we can forgive the creator of Vindici any deficiency on this score as freely as we forgive anything to the creators of Orlando Friscobaldo and Sir Giles Over-reach.

It is not so easy, however, to overlook or excuse his pointed and superfluous allusions to certain nameless and detestable abominations to which his countrymen were for the most part strangers, and which our noble and manly literature has systematically passed over with the contemptuous silence they deserve. Marston may be forgiven, and something may be conceded to Churchill, though even satire should fly at something higher than carrion, and at nothing lower than humanity. But enough.

Eleven stanzas crown Sappho for ever peerless queen of the lyre strung by Erato ; a few disjointed fragments sufficed to satisfy Goethe that in Menander perished the supreme genius of grace and symmetry ; on five hundred and twenty lines rests unshaken the fame of Persius ; and the composition of a single play enthrones Tourneur among the

lords of English tragedy. Without being insensible
to the splendid, impressive, and elaborate work of
Beaumont and Ford, so minutely and eloquently
interpreted to us by Mr. Swinburne's Essays, we
must certainly rank together the "Duchess of
Malfi," "Vittoria Corombona," and the "Revenger's
Tragedy" as the noblest and worthiest of the many
offerings laid by rapt disciples at the feet of their
common master—Shakespeare. The play has many
defects, no doubt ; of some of them I have already
spoken ; with respect to others, they lie principally
in the delineation of the subordinate characters, who
want colour and complexity. Hippolito, for instance, is a mere shadow; Ambitioso and Super-
vacuo are simply what their names imply, they are
not men so much as abstractions ; they enact a
set part, and reveal no capabilities for anything
else. Castiza never appears except to assert or
defend her chastity, a treasure much too cheap, and
necessarily, to justify her wearisome eulogies. There
is something unsatisfactory and unpleasantly rapid
about the change in the character and position of
the mother, though her repentance at the dagger's
edge probably left her as base as it found her—but
Tourneur should have marked it. The action of the
play sometimes flags when it should hurry on, and
sometimes hurries on when it might with advantage
slacken its pace. But through this chaos of bleared,

rapid, and uneven work spring into fierce and vivid light a series of scenes and positions unique in conception, brilliant and powerful in execution. The opening scene, with the torch-light flaring on the blood-stained, lust-rotted, hellish crew, as they pass over the stage, hearing not nor heeding the Revenger, the trial of the younger brother, the scene between the Duchess and Spurio, the scenes between Castiza and her mother, between Vindici, his mother, and sister, between the brothers and their mother, the murder of the Duke, the scene at the feast—some of these are of an excellence almost unapproachable ; all of them may rank among the most graphic and impressive passages in the whole body of our drama. The character of Vindici in its appalling and unrelieved intensity, in its savage and devilish energy, bitter cynicism, and angry grandeur, is unrivalled among the creations of an age which abounds in similar portraits. The Duke, the Duchess, and the younger brother are all masterly sketches, vigorously conceived and admirably sustained.

High among Tourneur's distinctive merits must also be ranked his singular mastery over the element of language. In graphic intensity of magical expression, he is second only to Shakespeare and Webster. He wields at will subtle, poignant phrase, curt, irritable turn, searching epithet, pregnant epigram, or, again, lucid, copious and expansive speech, rising and falling in easy and exquisite harmony with the thought it expresses.   In words which burn like fire and brand like vitriol, Vindici clothes his scoffs and mockery ; in words which melt like music, Castabella mourns her young lover or pleads with her unnatural step-father.   His versification also is, like Shakespeare's on which it is carefully formed, much wider in its range and varied in its mould than is usual with his contemporaries, whose styles are, so far at least as essential attributes are concerned, comparatively uniform and manneristic.   I question, for instance, whether two passages, so intrinsically different in form and rhythm as the following, could be selected from any other single author of that age with the exception of Shakespeare :

> " Here's an eye
> Able to tempt a great man to serve God ;
> A pretty hanging lip that has forgot now to dissemble ;
> Methinks this mouth should make a swearer tremble,
> A drunkard claspe his teeth and not undo 'em
> To suffer wet damnation to run through 'em.
> Here's a cheek keeps her colour, let the wind go whistle ;
> Spout, rain, we fear thee not ; be hot or cold,
> All's one with us."

And—

> " O doe not wrong him !   Tis a generous mind
> That ledde his disposition to the warre :
> For gentle love and noble courage are
> So near allied, that one begets another ;
> Or Love is sister and Courage is the brother.

Could I affect him better than before
His soldier's heart would make me love him more.
  *   *   *   *   *   *   *   *
    Though young depriv'd of breath,
He did not suffer an untimely death ;
But we may say of his brave blessed decease
' He died in war, and yet he died in peace.' "

Could verse be more various in cast and rhythm ? could verse be more perfect in the several and dissimilar elements which constitute its perfection ? Another striking and distinctive feature in his work is the boldness, felicity, and originality of his imagery and trick of putting things. I would instance such :

" To have her train borne up, and her soul traile i' the dirt."
        Revenger's Tragedy, act iv.

" Let our two other hands teare up his lids
And make his eyes, like Comets, shine through blood."
        Id., act iii.

" I have endur'd you with an ear of fire ;
Your tongues have struck hot irons in my face :
Mother, come from that poisonous woman there."—*Id.*, act ii.

" Slaves are but nails to drive out one another."—*Id.*, act v.

    " I could scarce
Kneel out my prayers, and had much ado
In three hours' reading to untwist so much
Of the black serpent as you wound about me."—*Id.*, act v.

     " On
The altar of his tomb I sacrifice
My teares. They are the jewels of my love
Dissolved into grief."—*Atheist's Tragedy*, act iii.

See, too, the whole of the beautiful passage in act

ii. of the same play, beginning, " Walking next day upon the fatal shore," etc.

" She's like your diamond, a temptation in every man's eye,
   Yet not yielding to any light and impression herself."– *Id.*, act i.

" The love of a woman is like a mushroom ; it grows in one night,
   and will serve somewhat pleasingly next morning to breakfast :
   but afterwards waxes fulsome and unwholesome."—*Id.*, act iii.

   " Patience is the honest man's revenge."—*Id.*, act v.

   " His mind was like an empire rich and strong
      In all defensive power."—*Poem on Sir Edward Vere.*

But enough of what every page will illustrate. The fierce and fiery splendour of his genius, the intensity of his envisaging and descriptive energy, and the imperial confidence he must have felt in his powers of high-pitched and sustained effort are nobly illustrated in the first scene of his great drama. With no gradual and tentative step does he glide, as others glide, consciously reservative into the current of his plot, but with one bound he has sprung into the very heart of his work ; is in the midst of his characters ; has discriminated and painted them ; has made the plot clear, the position of the principal figure definite, and the whole action of the piece setting swiftly towards the catastrophe. But these same attributes have occasionally betrayed him into the hurried, rugged, and careless work which sometimes disfigures his pages. They have contributed also to form a marked feature in his style, and have in the same way had a deteriorating, as well as a beneficial influence upon it. They are the fruitful source, not only of the daring and felicitous terseness which points and vivifies, but of the obscurities also which mar and perplex his diction.

This cramped and unpleasant condensation is sometimes carried so far that one is inclined very often to suspect that there must be some corruption in the text. A little reflection will, however, often show that it simply arises from excessive brevity. For this he found a precedent in Shakespeare, as there are no traces in his works of any knowledge either of Tacitus or Dante, though he might have recognised in both of them some strange resemblances to himself. As instances of this obscure and excessive brevity, we may take one or two passages in the "Revenger's Tragedy":

> "*Vind.* How don you? God you god-den.
> *Luss.* We thank thee.
> How strangely such a coarse homely salute
> Shows in the palace, where we greet in fire,
> Nimble and desperate tongues, should we name
> God in a salutation, 'twould ne'er be stood out—heaven!
> Tell me what made thee so melancholy?"

Or again:

> * "Too miserably great, rich to be eternally wretched;"

---

* Perhaps we should read "to be" instead of "too."

d—2

and again :

> "The mother's curse is heavy ; where that fights,
> Sonnes set in stormes, and daughters lose their lights ;"

and again :

> " Old men lustful
> Do show like young men, eager, violent ;
> Outbid like their limited performances."

Tourneur's great defect as a dramatic poet is undoubtedly the narrowness of his range of vision—of his insight and sympathies—and this is evident in the sketchy and abstract nature of many of his subordinate characters. Even D'Amville, the hero of the "Atheist's Tragedy," finely conceived, is very inadequately sustained, and fades at last into mere burlesque. His four principal female figures, Castabella, Castiza, Levidulcia, and Gratiana, differ merely in name, and what slight difference there is between them would seem to arise simply from the difference of the circumstances in which they are placed. They are even grouped similarly. Levidulcia and Gratiana, cast in the same mould, have pretty much the same character, and Castabella assumes the same attitude towards Levidulcia in the one play as Castiza assumes towards Gratiana in the other. None of his dramatis personæ are at all complex ; they are either the personifications of certain attributes—tragic studies of tragic humours, as Ben Jonson's masterpieces are comic studies of comic humours—or they are abstractions, phantoms, failures. He has apparently noticed the former peculiarity himself, and been careful to mark it in the nomenclature adopted for his characters. It is curious also to observe that where his names are not thus allegorically coined they are almost without exception borrowed from contemporary dramas.

In closing our review of these works it is difficult to leave them without pausing for a moment over the memóry of their author, who, with obvious but perhaps unconscious egotism, has evidently left in their strange and melancholy pages no inconsiderable fragments of his own strange and melancholy autobiography. Of his life among men, of his struggles and vicissitudes, not a trace, as we have seen, remains; but of that inner life, which is the soul of action, and is all that can interest or concern any one when the grave has closed over the actor, we cannot but feel that the veil has been uplifted, and that these two plays have other than mere literary fascination. Nothing, it is true, is so idle, so easy, and so presumptuous as to speculate and theorise on subjects like these; but here it is no officious recreation, but an imperative duty, with such lyric intensity and passionate abandonment has a poet stamped on his writings the terrible traces of so much bitter experience, of so much suffering, cynicism, and despair. Never, indeed,

with the single exception of Byron, has a dramatist,
while preserving successfully a certain superficial
and technical consistency in the delineation of subordinate characters altogether out of the range of
his care, comprehension, and sympathy, so obviously
and so defiantly interwoven and interpenetrated
objective embodiment with an intense all-absorbing
subjectivity. Dramatic more in form than spirit,
in particular detail rather than in general conception, these two plays have the same dreary burden,
the same melancholy moral, and in all the various
speeches of their many actors rings out the same
hollow laughter, or falters low the same hopeless
pathos. One chord is struck and there are no variations ; one tale is told and there are no episodes.
But how deep and piercing is the note, how savage
and significant the burden ! It is the egotism of a
powerful and distorted mind, which narrowed as it
hardened and gained in intellectual vigour as it lost
in sensuality and enthusiasm. It would seem that
he united the not uncommon anomaly of a fiery
and restless soul with a cold and logical intellect.
Where such a perilous union, no longer mutually
corrective, fails to secure in consistent purpose the
principle of healthy and harmonious actions, or to
find at all events a narcotic in the possession of
humour, it must either work its own speedy destruction, or, tortured into morbid and irritable

action, become the fruitful parent of " all monstrous, all abhorred things."

Nature, who had in many respects endowed him so richly, had altogether denied him this sense of humour, and consequently the balance and insight which humour is usually able to bestow. Hence, no doubt, the diseased, warped, and chaotic character of much of his work.

The incidents and struggles of his personal life probably differed little from those of two-thirds of his fellow-dramatists, among whom it would seem he had not received the recognition to which his genius certainly entitled him. All this operating on a man of his exceptional and peculiar temperament, of his sullen, unsocial and retiring disposition, would naturally make him what he appears to have been, so far at least as we can read his character from his writings. In the lonely laboratory of self he worked out his theory of the world-drama evolving round him, and flung his indignant transcript for all to read and some to understand—and a melancholy page it is. Man is not with him the creature of mixed motives, nor life the battle-ground between alternating light and darkness. It is the dreary stage on which Vindicis, Lussuriosos, Borachios, Soquettes, Cataplasmas, D'Amvilles, Snuffes, Levidulcias, Gratianas and Spurios are to sin their barren sins, or Castizas, Antonios, Montferrers, and

Sebastians to drain the cup of their aimless and grotesque sufferings for the amusement of the mocking
beholder and expectant hell.   Like Marlowe, he
hungers and thirsts after the sensuous, the defiant
and the forbidden, but he has none of Marlowe's
glory, grandeur and idealism.   Like Webster, he
loves to live among horrors till he has become
" native and endowed unto that element ;" but he
moves not with the same firm tread through tangled
labyrinths of gloom and wreck with " Look you, the
stars shine still !" as creed at once and comment.
Sin and misery, lust and cynicism, fixed their fangs
deep in his splendid genius, marring and defacing
his art, poisoning and paralysing the artist.   But
his life's work, such as it was, was complete and
consistent, and it is not the province of criticism
either to regret what is or to speculate about what
might have been.   That he perished prematurely
while passing through a stage which is with most
men of genius essentially transitory can scarcely
be conjectured with any confidence, for crude and
bitter as his philosophy of life may seem, its crudeness is not the crudeness of immaturity, or its bitterness the sort of bitterness which a wider experience would have been likely to sweeten.

THE

ATHEIST'S
TRAGEDIE:

or,

The honest Man's Reuenge.

As in diuers places it hath often beene Acted.

Written

By *Cyril Tourneur.*

AT LONDON,

Printed for *John Stepneth*, and *Richard Redmer*,
and are to be sold at their Shops at
the West End of Paules.

1611

The names and qualities of the Actors.

Montferrers, a Baron.

Belforest, a Baron.

D'amville, brother to *Mont-ferrers*.

Leuidulcia, Lady to *Belforest*.

Castabella, Daughter to *Bel-forest*.

Charlemont, sonne to *Mont-ferrers*.

Rousard, elder Sonne to *D'amville*.

Sebastian, younger sonne to *D'amville*.

Languebeau Snuffe, a Puri-tane ; Chaplaine to *Bel-forest*.

Borachio, *D'amville's* in-strument.

Cataplasma, a maker of Periwigges and Attires.

Soquette, a seeming Gentle-woman to *Cataplasma*.

Fresco, Seruant to *Cata-plasma*.

Other seruants.

Serieant in warre.

Souldiers.

Watchmen.

Officers.

Judges.

THE

ATHEIST'S TRAGEDIE.

ACTUS PRIMI   SCENA PRIMA

Enter D'AMUILLE, BORACHIO, *attended.*

D'amuille.

SAW my Nephew Charlemont but now
  Part from his Father. Tell him I desire
  To speake with him. *Exit* SERUANT.
Borachio, thou art read
In Nature and her large Philosophie.
Obseru'st thou not the very selfe same course
Of reuolution, both in Man and Beast?

Bor. The same, for birth, growth, state, decay and
   death ;
  Onely a man's beholding to his Nature
  For th' better composition o' the two.

D'am. But where that fauour of his Nature is
　　　Not full and free, you see a man becomes
　　　A foole, as little-knowing as a beast.

　Bor. That showes there's nothing in a Man aboue
　　　His nature ; if there were, consid'ring 'tis
　　　His being's excellencie, 'twould not yeeld
　　　To Nature's weakenesse.

D'am. Then, if Death casts up
　　　Our totall summe of joy and happinesse,
　　　Let me haue all my sences feasted in
　　　Th' abundant fulnesse of delight at once,
　　　And, with a sweet insensible increase
　　　Of pleasing surfet, melt into my dust.

　Bor. That reuolution is too short, me thinkes.
　　　If this life comprehends our happinesse,
　　　How foolish to desire to dye so soone !
　　　And if our time runnes home unto the length
　　　Of Nature, how improuident it were
　　　To spend our substance on a minute's pleasure,
　　　And after, liue an age in miserie !

D'am. So thou conclud'st that pleasure onely flowes

　　　Upon the streame of riches ?

Bor. Wealth is Lord
     Of all felicitie.

D'am. 'Tis, Oracle.
     For what's a man that's honest without wealth ?

Bor. Both miserable and contemptible.

D'am. Hee's worse, Borachio.   For if Charitie
     Be an essentiall part of Honestie,
     And should be practis'd first upon our selues,
     Which must be graunted, then your honest man
     That's poore, is most dishonest, for hee is
     Uncharitable to the man whom hee
     Should most respect.   But what doth this touch me
     That seeme to haue enough?—thankes industrie.
     'Tis true, had not my Body spredde it selfe
     Into posteritie, perhaps I should
     Desire no more increase of substance, then
     Would hold proportion with mine owne dimen-
         tions.
     Yet euen in that sufficiencie of state,
     A man has reason to prouide and adde.
     For what is he hath such a present eye,
     And so prepar'd a strength, that can fore-see,
     And fortifie his substance and himselfe

Against those accidents, the least whereof
May robbe him of an age's husbandry?
And for my children, they are as neere to me
As branches to the tree whereon they grow;
And may as numerously be multiplied.
As they increase, so should my prouidence;
For from my substance they receiue the sap,
Whereby they liue and flowrish.

Bor. Sir, enough.
I understand the marke whereat you aime.

Enter CHARLEMONT.

D'am. Silence, w'are interrupted.   Charlemont!

Char. Good morrow, Uncle.

D'am. Noble Charlemont,
Good morrow.   Is not this the honour'd day
You purpos'd to set forward to the warre?

Char. My inclination did intend it so.

D'am. And not your resolution?

Char. Yes, my Lord;
Had not my Father contradicted it.

D'am. O noble warre!   Thou first originall

Of all man's honour, how dejectedly
The baser Spirit of our present time
Hath cast it selfe below the ancient worth
Of our forefathers ! From whose noble deedes
Ignobly we deriue our pedigrees.

Charl. Sir, taxe not me for his unwillingnesse.
By the command of his authoritie
My disposition's forc'd against it selfe.

D'am. Nephew, you are the honour of our bloud.
The troope of Gentry, whose inferiour worth
Should second your example, are become
Your Leaders ; and the scorne of their discourse
Turnes smiling backe upon your backwardnesse.

Charl. You neede not urge my spirit by disgrace,
'Tis free enough ; my Father hinders it.
To curbe me, hee denyes me maintenance
To put me in the habite of my ranque.
Unbinde me from that strong necessitie,—
And call me Coward, if I stay behind.

D'am. For want of meanes ? Borachio, where's the gold ?
I'de disinherite my posteritie
To purchase honour.   'Tis an interest
I prize aboue the principall of wealth.

I'm glad I had th' occasion to make knowne
How readily my substance shall unlocke
It selfe to serue you. Here's a thousand Crownes.

Charl. My worthy uncle, in exchange for this
I leaue my bond; so I am doubly bound;
By that, for the repayment of this gold,
And by this gold, to satisfie your loue.

D'am. Sir, 'tis a witnesse onely of my loue,
And loue doth alwayes satisfie it selfe.
Now to your Father, labour his consent,
My importunitie shall second yours.
Wee will obtaine it.

Charl. If intreatie faile,
The force of reputation shall preuaile.   *Exit.*

D'am. Goe call my sonnes, that they may take their leaues
Of noble Charlemont.   Now, my Borachio !

Bor. The substance of our former argument
Was wealth.

D'am. The question, how to compasse it.

Bor. Young Charlemont is going to the warre.

D'am. O, thou begin'st to take me !

Bor. Marke me then.

Me thinkes the pregnant wit of Man might make
The happy absence of this Charlemont
A subiect of commodious prouidence.
He has a wealthy Father, ready eu'n
To drop into his graue.   And no man's power,
When Charlemont is gone, can interpose
'Twixt you and him.

D'am. Th'ast apprehended both
My meaning and my loue.   Now let thy trust,
For undertaking and for secrecie
Hold measure with thy amplitude of wit ;
And thy reward shall parallel thy worth.

Bor. My resolution has already bound
Mee to your seruice.

D'am. And my heart to thee.

Enter ROUSARD *and* SEBASTIAN.
Here are my Sonnes. ————
There's my eternitie.   My life in them
And their succession shall for euer liue.
And in my reason dwels the prouidence
To adde to life as much of happinesse.
Let all men lose, so I increase my gaine,
I haue no feeling of another's paine.   *Exeunt.*

[SCENE II.]

Enter OLD MONTFERRERS *and* CHARLEMONT.

Mont. I prithee, let this current of my teares
Diuert thy inclination from the warre,
For of my children thou art onely left
To promise a succession to my house.
And all the honour thou canst get by armes
Will giue but vaine addition to thy name ;
Since from thy auncestours thou dost deriue
A dignitie sufficient, and as great
As thou hast substance to maintaine and beare.
I prithee, stay at home.

Charl. My noble Father,
The weakest sigh you breathe hath power to turne
My strongest purpose, and your softest teare
To melt my resolution to as soft
Obedience ; but my affection to the warre
Is as hereditary as my bloud
To eu'ry life of all my ancestry.
Your predecessours were your presidents,
And you are my example.   Shall I serue
For nothing but a vaine Parenthesis

I' th' honour'd story of your Familie?
Or hang but like an emptie Scutcheon
Betweene the trophees of my predecessours,
And the rich Armes of my posteritie?
There's not a French-man of good bloud and
    youth,
But either out of spirit or example
Is turn'd a Souldier.   Onely Charlemont
Must be reputed that same heartlesse thing
That Cowards will be bold to play upon.

   Enter D'AMVILLE, ROUSARD, *and* SEBASTIAN.

D'am. Good morrow, my Lord.

Mont. Morrow, good brother.

Charl. Good morrow, Uncle.

D'am. Morrow, kinde Nephew.
   What, ha' you washed your eyes wi' teares this
      morning?
    Come, by my soule, his purpose does deserue
    Your free consent;—your tendernesse disswades
      him.
    What to the Father of a Gentleman
    Should be more tender then the maintenance

And the increase of honour to his house ?
My Lord, here are my Boyes.   I should be proud
That either this were able, or that inclin'd
To be my Nephewe's braue competitor.

Mont. Your importunities haue ouercome.
Pray God my forc'd graunt proue not ominous !

D'am. We haue obtain'd it.—Ominous ! in what ?
It cannot be in any thing but death.
And I am of a confident beliefe
That eu'n the time, place, manner of our deathe,
Doe follow Fate with that necessitie
That makes us sure to dye.   And in a thing
Ordain'd so certainly unalterable,
What can the use of prouidence preuaile ?

Enter BELFOREST, LEUIDULCIA, CASTABELLA, *attended.*

Bel. Morrow, my Lord Montferrers, Lord D'amville.
Good morrow, Gentlemen.   Couzen Charlemont,
Kindly good morrow.   Troth, I was afear'd
I should ha' come too late to tell you that
I wish your undertakings a successe
That may deserue the measure of their worth.

Char. My Lord, my dutie would not let me goe

Without receiuing your commandëments.

Bel. Accomplements are more for ornament
    Then use. Wee should imploy no time in them
    But what our serious businesse will admit.

Mont. Your fauour had by his duty beene preuented,
    If we had not with-held him in the way.

D'am. Hee was a coming to present his seruice ;
    But now no more. The booke inuites to breakfast.
    Wilt please your Lordship enter ?—Noble Lady !

    Manent CHARLEMONT *and* CASTABELLA.

Charl. My noble Mistresse, this accomplement
    Is like an elegant and mouing speech,
    Compos'd of many sweete perswasiue points,
    Which second one another, with a fluent
    Increase and confirmation of their force,
    Reseruing still the best untill the last,
    To crowne the strong impulsion of the rest
    With a full conquest of the hearer's sense :
    Because th' impression of the last we speake
    Doth alwayes longest and most constantly
    Possesse the entertainment of remembrance ;
    So all that now salute my taking leaue

Haue added numerously to the loue
Wherewith I did receiue their courtesie.
But you, deare Mistresse, being the last and best
That speakes my farewell, like th' imperious close
Of a most sweete Oration, wholy haue
Possess'd my liking, and shall euer liue
Within the soule of my true memory.
So, Mistresse, with this kisse I take my leaue.

Casta. My worthy Seruant, you mistake th' intent
Of kissing.   'Twas not meant to separate
A paire of Louers, but to be the seale
Of Loue ; importing by the joyning of
Our mutuall and incorporated breaths,
That we should breathe but one contracted life.
Or stay at home, or let me goe with you.

Charl. My Castabella, for my selfe to stay,
Or you to goe, would either taxe my youth
With a dishonourable weakenesse, or
Your louing purpose with immodestie.

Enter LANGUEBEAU SNUFFE.

And, for the satisfaction of your loue,
Heere comes a man whose knowledge I haue
        made

A witnesse to the contract of our vowes,

Which my returne, by marriage, shall confirme.

Lang. I salute you both with the spirit of copulation,

already informed of your matrimoniall pur-

poses, and will testimonie to the integritie—

Casta. O the sad trouble of my fearefull soule!

My faithfull seruant, did you neuer heare

That when a certaine great man went to th' warre,

The louely face of heauen was masqu'd with sorrow,

The sighing windes did moue the breast of earth,

The heauie cloudes hung downe their mourning

heads,

And wept sad showers the day that hee went

hence;

As if that day presag'd some ill successe

That fatallie should kill his happinesse.

And so it came to passe. Me thinkes my eyes

(Sweet Heau'n forbid!) are like those weeping

cloudes,

And as their showers presag'd, so doe my teares.

Some sad euent will follow my sad feares.

Charl. Fie, superstitious! Is it bad to kisse?

Casta. May all my feares hurt me no more then this!

Lang. Fie, fie, fie ! these carnall kisses doe stirre up the
    Concupiscences of the flesh.

    Enter BELFOREST *and* LEUIDULCIA.

Leuid. O ! here's your daughter under her seruant's lips.

Charl. Madame, there is no cause you should mistrust
    The kisse I gaue ; 'twas but a parting one.

Leuid. A lustie bloud !   Now by the lip of Loue,
    Were I to choose your joyning one for mee—

Bel. Your Father stayes to bring you on the way.
    Farewell.   The great Commander of the warre
    Prosper the course you undertake !   Farewell.

Charl. My Lord, I humbly take my leaue.—Madame,
    I kisse your hand.—And your sweet lip.—Fare-
    well.   [Farewell.

                                    Exeunt.

    Manent CHARLEMONT *and* LANGUEBEAU.

Her power to speake is perish'd in her teares.
Something within me would perswade my stay,
But Reputation will not yeeld unto't.
Dear Sir, you are the man whose honest trust
My confidence hath chosen for my friend.
I feare my absence will discomfort her.

You haue the power and opportunitie
To moderate her passion.   Let her griefe
Receiue that friendship from you, and your Loue
Shall not repent itselfe of courtesie.

Lang. Sir, I want words and protestation to insinuate
into your credit ; but in plainnesse and truth,
I will qualifie her griefe with the spirit of
consolation.

Charl. Sir, I will take your friendship up at use,
And feare not that your profit shall be small ;
Your interest shall exceede your principall.

Exit CHARL.

Enter D'AMVILLE *and* BORACHIO.

D'am. Monsieur Languebeau ! happily encountered. The
honestie of your conuersation makes me request more int'rest in your familiaritie.

Lang. If your Lordship will be pleased to salute me without ceremonie, I shall be willing to exchange
my seruice for your fauour ; but this worship-
ping kinde of entertainment is a superstitious
vanitie ; in plainnesse and truth, I loue it not.

D'am. I embrace your disposition, and desire to giue

2—2

you as liberall assurance of my loue as my
Lord Belforest, your deserued fauourer.

Lang. His Lordship is pleased with my plainnesse and
truth of conuersation.

D'am. It cannot displease him.   In the behauiour of his
noble daughter Castabella a man may read
her worth and your instruction.

Lang. That Gentlewoman is most sweetly modest, faire,
honest, handsome, wise, well-borne, and rich.

D'am. You haue giuen me her picture in small.

Lang. She's like your Dyamond; a temptation in euery
man's eye, yet not yeelding to any light impression her selfe.

D'am. The praise is hers, but the comparison your owne.
                              Gives him the Ring.

Lang. You shall forgiue me that, Sir.

D'am. I will not doe so much at your request as forgiue
you it.   I will onely giue you it, Sir.   By
—— You will make me sweare.

Lang. O ! by no meanes.   Prophane not your lippes with
the foulnesse of that sinne.   I will rather take
it.   To saue your oath, you shall lose your

Ring.—Verily, my Lord, my praise came short
of her worth.   She exceedes a Jewell.   This
is but onely for ornament : she both for ornament and use.

D'am. Yet unprofitably kept without use.   Shee deserues
a worthy Husband, Sir.   I haue often wish'd
a match betweene my elder sonne and her.
The marriage would joyne the houses of
Belforest and D'amville into a noble alliance.

Lang. And the unitie of Families is a worke of loue and
charitie.

D'am. And that worke an imployment well becomming
the goodnesse of your disposition.

Lang. If your Lordship please to impose it upon mee, I
will carry it without any second end ; the
surest way to satisfie your wish.

D'am. Most   joyfully   accepted.—*Rousard !*   Here are
Letters to my Lord Belforest, touching my
desire to that purpose.

Enter ROUSARD *sickely.*

Rousard, I send you a suitor to Castabella.   To
this Gentleman's discretion I commit the

managing of your suite. His good successe
shall be most thankefull to your trust. Follow
his instructions ; he will be your leader.

Lang. In plainnesse and truth.

Rous. My leader ! Does your Lordship thinke mee too
weake to giue the on-set my selfe ?

Lang. I will onely assist your proceedings.

Rous. To say true, so I thinke you had neede ; for a
sicke man can hardly get a woman's good
will without help.

Lang. Charlemont, thy gratuitie and my promises were
both
But words, and both, like words, shall vanish into
ayre.
For thy poore empty hand I must be mute ;
This giues mee feeling of a better suite.

                    Exeunt LANGUEBEAU *and* ROUSARD.

D'am. Borachio, didst precisely note this man ?

Bor. His owne profession would report him pure.

D'am. And seemes to knowe if any benefit
Arises of religion after death.
Yet but compare 's profession with his life ;—

They so directly contradict themselues,
As if the end of his instructions were
But to diuert the world from sinne, that hee
More easily might ingrosse it to himselfe.
By that I am confirm'd an Atheist.
Well ! Charlemont is gone ; and here thou seest
His absence the foundation of my plot.

Bor. Hee is the man whom Castabella loues.

D'am. That was the reason I propounded him
Employment, fix'd upon a forraine place,
To draw his inclination out o' th' way.

Bor. 'Thas left the passage of our practise free.

D'am. This Castabella is a wealthy heire ;
And by her marriage with my elder Sonne
My house is honour'd and my state increas'd.
This worke alone deserues my industry ;
But if it prosper, thou shalt see my braine
Make this but an induction to a point
So full of profitable policie,
That it would make the soule of honestie
Ambitious to turne villaine.

Bor. I bespeake
Employment in 't.   I'le be an instrument

To grace performance with dexteritie.

D'am. Thou shalt. No man shall rob thee of the honour.

Goe presently and buy a crimson Scarfe

Like Charlemont's : prepare thee a disguise

I' th' habite of a Soldiour, hurt and lame ;

And then be ready at the wedding feast,

Where thou shalt haue imployment in a worke

Will please thy disposition.

Bor. As I vow'd,

Your instrument shall make your project proud.

D'am. This marriage will bring wealth. If that succeede,

I will increase it though my Brother bleed.

Exeunt.

[SCENE III.]

Enter CASTABELLA *auoiding the importunitie of* ROUSARD.

Casta. Nay, good Sir ; in troth if you knew how little it

pleases mee, you would forbeare it.

Rous. I will not leaue thee till thou 'st entertain'd mee

for thy seruant.

Casta. My seruant ! You are sicke you say. You would

taxe mee of indiscretion to entertaine one that is not able to doe me seruice.

Rous. The seruice of a Gentlewoman consists most in chamber worke, and sicke men are fittest for the chamber. I pri'thee giue me a fauour.

Casta. Mee thinkes you haue a very sweet fauour of your owne.

Rous. I lacke but your blacke eye.

Casta. If you goe to buffets among the Boyes, they 'll giue you one.

Rous. Nay, if you grow bitter Ill dispraise your blacke eye. The gray eie'd Morning makes the fairest day.

Casta. Now that you dissemble not, I could be willing to giue you a fauour. What fauour would you haue?

Rous. Any toy, any light thing.

Casta. Fie! Will you be so unciuill to aske a light thing at a Gentlewoman's hand?

Rous. Wilt giue me a bracelet o' thy haire then?

Casta. Doe you want haire, Sir.

Rous. No faith, I'll want no haire, so long as I can haue it for mony.

Casta. What would you doe with my haire then?

Rous. Weare it for thy sake, sweet hart.

Casta. Doe you thinke I loue to haue my haire worne
off?

Rous. Come, you are so witty now and so sensible.

Kisses her.

Casta. Tush, I would I wanted one o' my sences now!

Rous. Bitter againe? What's that? Smelling?

Casta. No, no, no. Why now y'are satisfied I hope. I
haue giuen you a fauour.

Rous. What fauour? A kisse? I pri'thee giue mee
another.

Casta. Shew mee that I gaue it you then.

Rous. How should I shew it?

Casta. You are unworthie of a fauour if you will not
bestow the keeping of it one minute.

Rous. Well, in plaine termes, dost loue mee? That's
the purpose of my coming.

Casta. Loue you? Yes, very well.

Rous. Giue mee thy hand upon 't.

Casta. Nay, you mistake mee. If I loue you very well I

must not loue you now.　For now y'are not
very well, y'are sicke.

Rous. This Equiuocation is for the jest now.

Casta. I speak 't as 'tis now in fashion, in earnest.　But
I shall not be in quiet for you I perceiue, till
I haue giuen you a fauour.　Doe you loue
mee?

Rous. With all my hart.

Casta. Then with all my hart I'll giue you a Jewell to
hang in your eare.— Harke yee—I can neuer
loue you.　　　　　　　　　　　　　　　*Exit.*

Rous. Call you this a Jewell to hange in mine eare?　'Tis
no light fauour, for I'll be sworne it comes
somewhat heauily to mee.　Well, I will not
leaue her for all this.　Mee thinkes it animates
a man to stand to 't, when a woman desires
to be rid of him at the first sight.　　*Exit.*

[SCENE IV.]

Enter BELFOREST *and* LANGUEBEAU SNUFFE.

Bel. I entertaine the offer of this match
With purpose to confirme it presently.
I haue already moou'd it to my daughter.

Her soft excuses sauour'd at the first,
Me-thought, but of a modest innocence
Of bloud, whose unmoou'd streame was neuer
    drawne
Into the current of affection.   But when I
Replyed with more familiar arguments,
Thinking to make her apprehension bold,—
Her modest blush fell to a pale dislike,
And shee refus'd it with such confidence,
As if shee had beene prompted by a loue
Inclining firmely to some other man ;
And in that obstinacie shee remaines.

Lang. Verily, that disobedience doth not become a
       Childe.   It proceedeth from an unsanctified
       libertie.   You will be accessarie to your owne
       dishonour if you suffer it.

Bel. Your honest wisedome has aduis'd mee well.
       Once more I'll moue her by perswasiue meanes.
       If shee resist, all mildenesse set apart,
       I will make use of my authoritie.

Lang. And instantly, lest fearing your constraint
       Her contrary affection teach her some
       Deuise that may preuent you.

Bel. To cut off eu'ry opportunitie
Procrastination may assist her with
This instant night shee shall be marryed.

Lang. Best.

Enter CASTABELLA.

Casta. Please it your Lordship, my mother attends
I' th' Gallerie, and desires your conference.

Exit BELFOREST.

This meanes I us'd to bring mee to your eare.

(*To* LANGUEBEAU.)

Time cuts off circumstance; I must be briefe.
To your integritie did Charlemont
Commit the contract of his loue and mine;
Which now so strong a hand seekes to diuide,
That if your graue aduice assist me not,
I shall be forc'd to violate my faith.

Lang. Since Charlemont's absence I haue waigh'd his loue
with the spirit of consideration; and in sin-
ceritie I finde it to be friuolous and vaine.
With-draw your respect; his affection de-
serueth it not.

Casta. Good sir, I know your heart cannot prophane

The holinesse you make profession of
With such a vitious purpose as to breake
The vow your owne consent did help to make.

Lang. Can he deserue your loue who in neglect
Of your delightfull conuersation and
In obstinate contempt of all your prayers
And teares, absents himselfe so far from your
Sweet fellowship, and with a purpose so
Contracted to that absence that you see
Hee purchases your separation with
The hazard of his bloud and life, fearing to want
Pretence to part your companies.—
'Tis rather hate that doth diuision moue.
Loue still desires the presence of his Loue.—
Verily hee is not of the Familie of Loue.

Casta. O doe not wrong him ! 'Tis a generous minde
That ledde his disposition to the warre :
For gentle loue and noble courage are
So neare allyed, that one begets another ;
Or Loue is Sister and Courage is the Brother.
Could I affect him better then before,
His Souldier's heartwould make me loue him more.

Lang. But, Castabella—   *Enter* LEUIDULCIA.

Leu. Tush, you mistake the way into a woman.
The passage lyes not through her reason but her
bloud.

Exit LANGUEBEAU. CASTABELLA *about to follow.*

Nay, stay! How wouldst thou call the childe,
That being rais'd with cost and tendernesse
To full habilitie of body and meanes,
Denies reliefe unto the parents who
Bestow'd that bringing up?

Casta. Unnaturall.

Leu. Then Castabella is unnaturall.
Nature, the louing mother of us all,
Brought forth a woman for her owne reliefe
By generation to reuiue her age;
Which, now thou hast habilitie and meanes
Presented, most unkindly dost deny.

Casta. Beleiue me, Mother, I doe loue a man.

Leu. Preferr'st th' affection of an absent Loue
Before the sweet possession of a man;
The barren minde before the fruitfull body,
Where our creation has no reference
To man but in his body, being made

Onely for generation ; which (unlesse
Our children can be gotten by conceit)
Must from the body come ?   If Reason were
Our counsellour, wee would neglect the worke
Of generation for the prodigall
Expence it drawes us too of that which is
The wealth of life.   Wise Nature, therefore, hath
Reseru'd for an inducement to our sence
Our greatest pleasure in that greatest worke ;
Which being offer'd thee, thy ignorance
Refuses, for th' imaginarie joy
Of an unsatisfied affection to
An absent man whose bloud once spent i' th' warre
Then hee 'll come home sicke, lame, and impotent,
And wed thee to a torment, like the paine
Of Tantalus, continuing thy desire
With fruitlesse presentation of the thing
It loues, still moou'd, and still unsatisfied.

Enter BELFOREST, D'AMVILLE, ROUSARD, SEBASTIAN,
        LANGUEBEAU, &c.

Bel. Now, Leuidulcia, hast thou yet prepar'd
      My Daughter's loue to entertaine this Man
      Her husband, here ?

Leu. I'm but her mother i' law ;
　　Yet if shee were my very flesh and bloud
　　I could aduise no better for her* good.

Rous. Sweet wife,
　　Thy joyful husband thus salutes thy cheeke

Casta. My husband ?   O ! I am betraid.——
　　Deare friend of Charlemont, your puritie
　　Professes a diuine contempt o' th' world ;
　　O be not brib'd by that you so neglect,
　　In being the world's hated instrument,
　　To bring a just neglect upon your selfe !—*Kneeles*
　　　from one to another.
　　Deare Father, let me but examine my
　　Affection.——Sir, your prudent iudgement can
　　Perswade your sonne that 'tis improuident
　　To marry one whose disposition he
　　Did ne'er obserue.——Good sir, I may be of
　　A nature so unpleasing to your minde,
　　Perhaps you 'll curse the fatall houre wherein
　　You rashly marryed me.

D'am. My Lord Belforest,

---

* The quarto drops the *her*.

I would not haue her forc'd against her choise.

Bel. Passion o' me, thou peeuish girle !   I charge
Thee by my blessing, and th' authoritie
I haue to claime th' obedience, marry him.

Casta. Now Charlemont !   O my presaging teares !
This sad euent hath follow'd my sad feares.

Seba. A rape, a rape, a rape !

Bel. How now !

D'am. What's that ?

Seba. Why what is 't but a Rape to force a wench
To marry, since it forces her to lie
With him she would not ?

Lang. Verily his Tongue is an unsanctified member.

Seba. Verily
Your grauitie becomes your perish'd soule
As hoary mouldinesse does rotten fruit.

Bel. Couzen, y' are both unciuill and prophane.

D'am. Thou disobedient villaine, get thee out of my sight.
Now, by my Soule, Ile plague thee for this rude-
nesse.

Bel. Come, set forward to the Church.   *Exeunt.*

    Manet SEBASTIAN.

Seba. And verifie the Prouerbe—The nearer the Church,
the further from God.—Poore wench ! For
thy sake may his habilitie die in his appetite,
that thou beest not troubled with him thou
louest not ! May his appetite moue thy desire
to another man, so hee shall helpe to make
himselfe Cuckold ! And let that man be one
that he payes wages to ; so thou shalt profit
by him thou hatest. Let the Chambers be
matted, the hinges oyl'd, the curtaine rings
silenced, and the chamber-maid hold her peace
at his owne request, that he may sleepe the
quietlier; and in that sleepe let him be soundly
cuckolded. And when hee knowes it, and
seekes to sue a diuorce, let him haue no other
satisfaction then this : *Hee lay by and slept :
the Law will take no hold of her because he
wink'd at it.* *Exit.*

ACTUS SECUNDI SCENA PRIMA

Musicke.   A banquet.   In the night.

Enter D'AMVILLE, BELFOREST, LEUIDULCIA, ROUSARD, CASTABELLA, LANGUEBEAU SNUFFE, *at one doore.   At the other doore* CATAPLASMA *and* SOQUETTE, *usher'd by* FRESCO.

Leuidulcia.

Mistresse Cataplasma, I expected you an houre since.

Cata. Certaine Ladies at my house, Madame, detain'd mee ; otherwise I had attended your Ladiship sooner.

Leu. Wee are beholding to you for your companie. My Lord, I pray you bid these Gentlewomen welcome ; they're my inuited friends.

D'am. Gentlewomen, y'are welcome.   Pray sit downe.

Leu. Fresco, by my Lord D'amville's leaue I prithee goe into the Buttry.   Thou shalt finde some o' my men there.   If they bid thee not welcome they are very Loggerheads.

Fres. If your Loggerheads will not, your Hoggesheads
shall, Madame, if I get into the Buttry.

Exit.

D'am. That fellowe's disposition to mirth should be our
present example.   Let's be graue and medi-
tate when our affaires require our seriousnes.
'Tis out of season to be heauily disposed.

Leu. We should be all wound up into the key of Mirth.

D'am. The Musicke there.

Bel. Where's my Lord Montferrers ?   Tell him here's
a roome attends him.   *Enter* MONTFERRERS.

Mont. Heauen giue your marriage that I am depriu'd of,
ioy !

D'am. My Lord Belforest, Castabella's nealth !

[D'AMVILLE *drinkes.*]

Set ope' the Sellar dores, and let this health
Goe freely round the house.—Another to
Your Sonne, my Lord ; to noble Charlemont—
Hee is a Souldier— Let the Instruments
Of warre congratulate his memorie.

Drums and trumpets.

Enter a SERUANT.

Ser. My Lord, here's one, i' th' habite of a Souldier,
saies hee is newly return'd from Ostend, and
has some businesse of import to speake.

D'am. Ostend ! let him come in.   My soule fore-tels
Hee brings the newes will make our Musicke full.
My brother's joy would doe't, and here comes hee
Will raise it.

Enter BORACHIO *disguised.*

Mont. O my spirit, it does disswade
My tongue to question him, as if it knew
His answere would displease.

D'am. Souldier, what newes ?
Wee heard a rumour of a blow you gaue
The Enemie.

Bor. 'Tis very true, my Lord.

Bel. Canst thou relate it ?

Bor. Yes.

D'am. I Prithee doe.

Bor. The Enemie, defeated of a faire
Aduantage by a flatt'ring strategem,

Plants all th' Artillerie against the Towne ;
Whose thunder and lightning made our bulwarkes
   shake
And threatned in that terrible report
The storme wherewith they meant to second it.
Th' assault was generall.   But, for the place
That promis'd most aduantage to be forc'd—
The pride of all their Army was drawne forth
And equally diuided into Front
And Rere. They march'd, and comming to a stand,
Ready to passe our Channell at an ebbe,
W' aduis'd it for our safest course, to draw
Our sluices up and mak't unpassable.
Our Governour oppos'd and suffered them
To charge us home e'en to the Rampier's foot.
But when their front was forcing up our breach
At push o' pike, then did his pollicie
Let goe the sluices, and trip'd up the heeles
Of the whole bodie of their troupe that stood
Within the violent current of the streame.
Their front, beleaguer'd 'twixt the water and
The Towne, seeing the floud was growne too deepe
To promise them a safe retreate, expos'd

The force of all their spirits, (like the last
Expiring gaspe of a strong harted man)
Upon the hazard of one charge, but were
Oppress'd, and fell.   The reste that could not
      swimme
Were onely drown'd ; but those that thought to
      scape
By swimming, were by murtherers that flank'd
The leuell of the floud, both drown'd and slaine.

D'am. Now, by my soule, Souldier, a braue seruice.

Mont. O what became of my deare Charlemont ?

Bor. Walking next day upon the fatall shore,
Among the slaughter'd bodies of their men
Which the full-stomack'd Sea had cast upon
The sands, it was m' unhappy chance to light
Upon a face, whose fauour when it liu'd,
My astonish'd minde inform'd me I had seene.
Hee lay in's Armour, as if that had beene
His Coffine ; and the weeping Sea, like one
Whose milder temper doth lament the death
Of him whom in his rage he slew, runnes up
The Shoare, embraces him, kisses his cheeke,
Goes backe againe, and forces up the Sandes

To burie him, and eu'rie time it parts
Sheds teares upon him, till at last (as if
It could no longer endure to see the man
Whom it had slaine, yet loath to leaue him) with
A kinde of unresolu'd unwilling pace,
Winding her waues one in another, like
A man that foldes his armes or wrings his hands
For griefe, ebb'd from the body, and descends
As if it would sinke downe into the earth,
And hide it selfe for shame of such a deede.

D'am. And, Souldier, who was this?

Mont. O Charlemont!

Bor. Your feare hath told you that, whereof my griefe
Was loath to be the messenger.

Casta. O God!   *Exit* CASTABELLA.

D'am. Charlemont drown'd! Why how could that be, since
It was the aduerse partie that receiued
The ouerthrow?

Bor. His forward spirit press'd into the front,
And being engag'd within the enemie
When they retreated through the rising streame,

I' the violent confusion of the throng
Was ouerborne, and perish'd in the floud.
And here's the sad remembrance of his life, — *The
    Scarfe.*
Which, for his sake, I will for euer weare.

Mont. Torment me not with witnesses of that
Which I desire not to beleiue, yet must.

D'am. Thou art a Scrichowle and dost come i' th' night
To be the cursed messenger of death.
Away ! depart my house or, by my soule,
You'll finde me a more fatall enemie
Then euer was Ostend.   Be gone ; dispatch !

Bor. Sir, 'twas my loue.

D'am. Your loue to vexe my heart
With that I hate ?
Harke, doe you heare, you knaue ?
O thou'rt a most delicate, sweete, eloquent villaine !
                                                        [Aside.

Bor. Was't not well counterfaited ?   [Aside.

D'am. Rarely. [Aside] Be gone.   I will not here reply.

Bor. Why then, farewell.   I will not trouble you.
                                                        Exit.

D'am. So.   The foundation's laid.   Now by degrees

                                     [Aside.

The worke will rise and soone be perfected.

O this uncertaine state of mortall man !

Bel. What then ?   It is th' ineuitable fate

Of all things underneath the Moone.

D'am. 'Tis true.

Brother, for health's sake ouercome your griefe.

Mont. I cannot, sir.   I am uncapable

Of comfort.   My turne will be next.   I feele

Myselfe not well.

D'am. You yeeld too much to griefe.

Lang. All men are mortall.   The houre of death is un-

certaine.   Age makes sicknesse the more

dangerous, and griefe is subiect to distrac-

tion.   You know not how soone you may be

depriu'd of the benefit of sense.   In my un-

derstanding, therefore,

You shall doe well if you be sicke to set

Your state in present order.   Make your will.

D'am. I haue my wish.   Lights for my Brother.

Mont. Ile withdraw a while,

And craue the honest counsell of this man.

Bel. With all my heart. I pray attend him, sir.

Exeunt MONTFERRERS *and* SNUFFE.

This next roome, please your Lordship.

D'am. Where you will.

Exeunt BELFOREST *and* D'AMVILLE.

Leuid. My Daughter's gone. Come sonne, Mistresse Cataplasma, come, wee'll up into her chamber. I'de faine see how she entertaines the expectation of her husband's bedfellowship.

Rou. 'Faith, howsoeuer shee entertaines it, I
Shall hardly please her ; therefore let her rest.

Leuid. Nay, please her hardly, and you please her best.

Exeunt.

[SCENE II.]

Enter 3 SERUANTS, *drunke, drawing in* FRESCO.

1. *Ser.* Boy ! fill some drinke, Boy.

Fresco. Enough, good Sir ; not a drop more by this light.

2. *Ser.* Not by this light ? Why then put out the candles and wee'l drinke i' the darke, and t'-to 't, old Boy.

Fres. No, no, no, no, no.

3. *Ser.* Why then take thy liquour. A health, Fresco.

                                        kneele.

Fres. Your health will make me sicke, sir.

1. *Ser.* Then 'twill bring you o' your knees, I hope, sir.

Fres. May I not stand and pledge it, sir ?

2. *Ser.* I hope you will doe as wee doe.

Fres. Nay then indeed I must not stand, for you cannot.

3. *Ser.* Well said, old boy.

Fres. Old boy ! you'l make me a young childe anon ; for
    if I continue this I shall scarce be able to goe
    alone.

1. *Ser.* My body is a weake as water, Fresco.

Fres. Good reason, sir. The beere has sent all the malt
    up into your braine and left nothing but the
    water in your body.

Enter D'AMVILLE *and* BORACHIO, *closely obseruing their
drunkennesse.*

D'am. Borachio, seest those fellowes ?

Bor. Yes, my Lord.

D'am. Their drunkennesse, that seemes ridiculous,

Shall be a serious instrument to bring
Our sober purposes to their successe.

Bor. I am prepar'd for th' execution, sir.

D'am. Cast off this habite and about it straight.

Bor. Let them drinke healthes and drowne their braines
i' the floud ;
I promise them they shall be pledg'd in bloud.

Exit.

1. *Ser.* You ha' left a damnable snuffe here.

2. *Ser.* Doe you take that in snuffe, sir ?

1. *Ser.* You are a damnable rogue then —— [*together by
th' eares.*]

D'am. Fortune, I honour thee.   My plot still rises
According to the modell of mine owne desires.
Lights for my Brother. —— What ha' you
drunke yourselues mad, you knaues ?

1. *Ser.* My Lord, the Jackes abus'd mee.

D'am. I thinke they are the Jackes indeed that haue
abus'd thee.   Dost heare ?   That fellow is a
proud knaue.   Hee has abus'd thee.   As
thou goest ouer the fields by-and-by in light-
ing my brother home, I'll tell thee what shalt

doe. Knocke him ouer the pate with thy
torch. I'll beare thee out in't.

1. *Ser.* I will singe the goose by this torch.   *Exit.*

To Second Servant.

D'am. Dost heare, fellow?   Seest thou that proud knaue.
I haue giuen him a lesson for his sawcinesse.
He's wronged thee.   I will tell thee what shalt doe:
As we goe ouer the fields by and by
Clap him sodainely o'er the coxecombe with
Thy torch.   I'll beare thee out in't.

2. *Ser.* I will make him understand as much.   *Exit.*

Enter LANGUEBEAU SNUFFE.

D'am. Now, Mounsieur Snuffe, what has my brother
done?

Lang. Made his will, and by that will made you his
heyre with this prouiso, that as occasion shall
hereafter moue him, he may reuoke, or alter it
when he pleases.

D'am. Yes.   Let him if he can.——I'll make it sure
From his reuoking.   *Aside.*

Enter MONTFERRERS *and* BELFOREST *attended with lights.*
Mont. Brother, now good night.

D'am. The skie is darke ; wee'll bring you o'er the
    fields.

Who can but strike, wants wisedome to main-
    taine ;

Hee that strikes safe and sure, has heart and
    braine.   *Exeunt.*

[SCENE III.]

Enter CASTABELLA *alone.*

Casta. O Loue, thou chast affection of the Soule,

Without th' adultrate mixture of the bloud,

That vertue, which to goodnesse addeth good,—

The minion of heauen's heart.   Heauen ! is't my
    fate

For louing that thou lou'st, to get thy hate,

Or was my Charlemont thy chosen Loue,

And therefore hast receiu'd him to thy selfe ?

Then I confesse thy anger's not unjust.

I was thy riuall.   Yet to be diuorc'd

From loue, has beene a punishment enough

(Sweete heauen !) without being marryed unto
    hate

Hadst thou beene pleas'd, O double miserie
Yet, since thy pleasure hath inflicted it,
If not my heart, my dutie shall submit.

Enter LEUIDULCIA, ROUSARD, CATAPLASMA, SOQUETTE,
and FRESCO *with a lanthorne.*

Leu. Mistresse Cataplasma, good night. I pray when
your Man has brought you home let him returne and light me to my house.

Cata. He shall instantly waite upon your Ladiship.

Leu. Good Mistresse Cataplasma! for my seruants are
all drunke, I cannot be beholding to 'em for
their attendance.

Exeunt CATAPLASMA, SOQUETTE, *and* FRESCO.

O here's your Bride!

Rous. And melancholique too, methinkes.

Leu. How can shee choose? Your sicknesse will
Distaste th' expected sweetnesse o' the night
That makes her heauie.

Rou. That should make her light.

Leu. Looke you to that.

Casta. What sweetnesse speake you of?
    The sweetnesse of the night consists in rest.

Rou. With that sweetnesse thou shalt be surely blest
    Unlesse my groning wake thee.   Doe not moane.

Leu. She'd rather you would wake, and make her grone.

Rou. Nay 'troth, sweete heart, I will not trouble thee.
    Thou shalt not lose thy maiden-head to-night.

Casta. O might that weaknesse euer be in force,
    I neuer would desire to sue divorce.

Rou. Wilt goe to bed?

Casta. I will attend you, sir.

Rou. Mother, good night.

Leu. Pleasure be your bed-fellow.

Exeunt ROUSARD *and* CASTABELLA.

Why sure their Generation was asleepe
When shee begot those Dormice, that shee made
Them up so weakely and imperfectly.
One wants desire, the t'other habilitie,
When my affection euen with their cold blouds
(As snow rubb'd through an actiue hand does make

The flesh to burne) by agitation is
Inflam'd, I could imbrace and entertaine
The ayre to coole it.

Enter SEBASTIAN.

Seba. That but mitigates
The heate ; rather imbrace and entertaine
A younger brother; he can quench the fire.

Leu. Can you so, sir? Now I beshrew your eare.
Why, bold Sebastian, how dare you approach
So neare the presence of your displeas'd Father?

Seba. Under the protection of his present absence.

Leu. Belike you knew he was abroad then?

Seba. Yes.
Let me encounter you so; I'll perswade
Your meanes to reconcile me to his loue.

Leu. Is that the way? I understand you not.
But for your reconcilement meete m' at home ;
I'll satisfie your suite.

Seba. Within this halfe-houre?

Exit SEBASTIAN.

Leu. Or within this whole houre. When you will.—

4—2

A lusty bloud ! has both the presence and spirit
of a man.   I like the freedome of his behauiour.
—Ho !—Sebastian ! Gone ?—Has set
My bloud o' boyling i' my veynes.   And now,
Like water poured upon the ground that mixes
It selfe with eu'ry moysture it meetes, I could
Clasp with any man.

Enter FRESCO *with a Lanthorne.*

O, Fresco, art thou come ?
If t'other faile, then thou art entertain'd.
Lust is a Spirit, which whosoe'er doth raise,
The next man that encounters boldly, layes.

                                        Exeunt.

[SCENE IV.]

Enter BORACHIO *warily and hastily over the Stage with a
stone in eyther hand.*

Bor. Such stones men use to raise a house upon
       But with these stones I goe to ruine one.

                                        Descends.

Enter two Seruants drunke fighting with their torches.

D'AMVILLE, MONTFERRERS, BELFOREST, *and* LANGUEBEAU
SNUFFE.

Bel. Passion o' me, you drunken knaues! You'l put
The lights out.

D'am. No, my Lord ; th' are but in jest.

1. *Ser.* Mine's out.

D'am. Then light it at his head,—that's light enough.—
'Fore God, th' are out. You drunken Rascals,
backe
And light 'em.

Bel. 'Tis exceeding darke. *[Exeunt Seruants].*

D'am. No matter ;
I am acquainted with the way. Your hand.
Lets easily walke. I'll lead you till they come.

Mont. My soule's opprest with griefe. 'T lies heauie at
My heart. O my departed Sonne, ere long
I shall be with thee !

D'AMVILLE *thrusts him downe into the grauell pit.*

D'am. Marry, God forbid !

Mont. O, o, o !

D'am. Now all the hoste of heauen forbid! Knaues!
        Rogues!

Bel. Pray God he be not hurt. Hee's fall'n into the
        grauell-pit.

D'am. Brother! deare brother! Rascals! villaines!
        knaues!

Enter the Seruants with lights.

Eternall darknesse damne you! come away!
Goe round about into the grauell pit,
And helpe my Brother up. Why what a strange
Unlucky night is this! Is 't not, my Lord?
I thinke that Dogge that howl'd the newes of
        griefe,
That fatall Scrichowle usher'd on this mischiefe.

Enter with the murdered body.

Lan. Mischiefe indeed, my Lord. Your Brother's
        dead!

Bel. Hee's dead?

Ser. Hee's dead!

D'am. Dead be your tongues! Drop out
        Mine eye-bals and let enuious Fortune pla

At tennis with 'em. Haue I liu'd to this ?
Malicious Nature, hadst thou borne me blinde,
Th'adst yet been something fauourable to me.
No breath ? no motion ? Prithee tell me, heauen,
Hast shut thine eye to winke at murther ; or
Hast put this sable garment on to mourne
At 's death ?
Not one poore sparke in the whole spatious skye
Of all that endlesse number would vouchsafe
To shine ?—You vize-royes to the King of
    Nature,
Whose constellations gouerne mortall births,
Where is that fatall Planet rul'd at his
Natiuitie ? that might ha' pleas'd to light him out,
As well as into the world, unlesse it be
Ashamèd I haue beene the instrument
Of such a good man's cursed destinie.—

Belf. Passion transports you. Recollect your selfe.
    Lament him not. Whether our deaths be good
    Or bad, it is not death, but life that tryes.
    Hee liu'd well ; therefore, questionlesse, well
    dyes.

D'am. I, 'tis an easie thing for him that has

    No paine, to talke of patience. Doe you thinke
    That Nature has no feeling?

Belf. Feeling? Yes.
    But has she purpos'd any thing for nothing?
    What good receiues this body by your griefe?
    Whether is 't more unnaturall, not to grieue
    For him you cannot help with it, or hurt
    Your selfe with grieuing, and yet grieue in vaine?

D'am. Indeede, had hee beene taken from mee like
    A piece o' dead flesh, I should neither ha' felt it
    Nor grieued for 't. But come hether, pray look
    heere.
    Behold the liuely tincture of his bloud!
    Neither the Dropsie nor the Jaundies in 't,
    But the true freshnesse of a sanguine red,
    For all the fogge of this blacke murdrous night
    Has mix'd with it. For any thing I know
    Hee might ha' liu'd till doomesday, and ha' done
    More good then either you or I. O Brother!
    He was a man of such a natiue goodnesse,
    As if Regeneration had beene given
    Him in his mother's wombe. So harmëless
    That rather then ha' trod upon a worme

Hee would ha' shun'd the way.
So deerely pittifull that ere the poore
Could aske his charity with dry eyes he gaue 'em
Reliefe wi' teares—with teares—yes, faith, with
    teares.

Belf. Take up the Corps. For wisedom's sake let reason
    fortifie this weakenesse.

D'am. Why, what would you ha' mee doe? Foolish Nature
    Will haue her course in spight o' wisedom. But
    I haue e'en done. All these wordes were
    But a great winde ; and now this showre of teares
    Has layd it, I am calme againe. You may
    Set forward when you will. I'll follow you
    Like one that must and would not.

Lang. Our opposition will but trouble him.

Belf. The griefe that melts to teares by itselfe is spent;
    Passion resisted growes more violent.

                               Exeunt.

      Manet D'AMVILLE. BORACHIO *ascends.*

D'am. Here's a sweete Comedie. 'T begins with *O*
    Dolentis and concludes with ha, ha, he !

Bor. Ha, ha, he !

D'am. O my eccho ! I could stand
Reuerberating this sweete musicall ayre,
Of joy till I had perish'd my sound lungs
With violent laughter. Lonely Night-Rauen,
Th'ast seiz'd a carkasse.

Bor. Put him out on's paine.
I lay so fitly underneath the bancke,
From whence he fell, that ere his falt'ring tongue
Could utter double Oo, I knock'd out's braines
With this faire Rubie, and had another stone,
Just of this forme and bignesse, ready ; that
I laid i' the broken skull upon the ground
For's pillow, against the which they thought he
    fell
And perish'd.

D'am. Upon this ground Ile build my Manour house ;
And this shall be the chiefest corner stone.

Bor. 'T has crowned the most judicious murder that
The braine of man was ere deliuer'd of.

D'am. I, Marke the plot. Not any circumstance
That stood within the reach of the designe

Of persons, dispositions, matter, time, or place
But by this braine of mine was made
An Instrumentall help ; ýet nothing from
Th' induction to th' accomplishment seem'd forc'd,
Or done o' purpose, but by accident.

Bor. First, my report that Charlemont was dead,
Though false, yet couer'd with a masque of truth.

D'am. I, and deliuer'd in as fit a time
When all our mindes so wholy were possess'd
With one affaire, that no man would suspect
A thought imploi'd for any second end.

Bor. Then the Precisian to be ready, when
Your brother spake of death, to moue his Will.

D'am. His businesse call'd him thither and it fell
Within his office unrequested to 't.
From him it came religiously, and sau'd
Our project from suspition which if I
Had mou'ed, had beene endanger'd.

Bor. Then your healths,
Though seeming bùt the ordinarie rites
And ceremonies due to festiuals——

D'am. Yet us'd by me to make the seruants drunke,—

An instrument the plot could not haue miss'd.

'Twas easie to set drunkards by the eares

They'd nothing but their torches to fight with

And when those lights were out——

Bor. Then darkenesse did

Protect the execution of the worke

Both from preuention and discouerie.

D'am. Here was a murther brauely carryed through

The eye of obseruation, unobseru'd.

Bor. And those that saw the passage of it made

The Instruments, yet knew not what they did.

D'am. That power of rule Philosophers ascribe

To him they call the Supreame of the starres

Making their influences gouernours

Of Sublunarie Creatures when themselves

Are senselesse of their operations.

                              [*Thunder and lightning.*]

What !

Dost start at thunder ?   Credit my beliefe

'Tis a meere effect of nature—an exhalation hot

And dry inuolued within a watrie vapour

I' the middle region of the ayre; whose coldnesse,

Congealing that thicke moysture to a cloud,

The angry exhalation, shut within
A prison of contrary qualitie,
Striues to be free and with the violent
Eruption ihrough the grossenesse of that cloud,
M; . this noyse we heare.

Bor. 'Tis a fearefull noyse.

D'am. 'Tis a braue noyse, and meethinkes
Graces our accomplish'd project as
A peale of Ordnance does a triumph.   It speakes
Encouragement.   Now Nature showes thee how
It fauour'd our performance, to forbeare
This noyse when we set forth, because it should
Not terrifie my brother's going home,
Which would have dash'd our purpose,—to for-
beare
This lightning in our passage least it should
Ha' warn'd him o' the pitfall.
Then propitious Nature winck'd
At our proceedings : now it doth expresse
How that forbearance fauour'd our successe.

Bor. You haue confirm'd mee.   For it followes well
That Nature, since her selfe decay doth hate,
Should fauour those that strengthen their estate.

D'am. Our next endeauour is, since on the false
　　　 Report that Charlemont is dead depends
　　　 The fabrique of the worke, to credit that
　　　 With all the countenance wee can.

　Bor. Faith, Sir,
　　　 Euen let his own inheritance, whereof
　　　 Y'aue dispossess'd him, countenance the act.
　　　 Spare so much out of that to giue him a
　　　 Solempnitie of funerall.　'Twill quit
　　　 The cost, and make your apprehension of
　　　 His death appeare more confident and true.

D'am. I'll take thy counsell.　Now farewell, blacke
　　　　 Night;
　　　 Thou beauteous Mistresse of a murderer.
　　　 To honour thee that hast accomplish'd all
　　　 I'll weare thy colours at his funerall　　*Exeunt.*

[SCENE V.]

Enter LEUIDULCIA *into her chamber mann'd by* FRESCO.

　Leu. Th'art welcome into my chamber, Fresco. Prithee
　　　 shut the dore. ——— Nay, thou mistakest me.
　　　 Come in and shut it.

Fres. 'Tis somewhat late, Madame.

Leu. No matter. I haue somewhat to say to thee. What, is not thy mistresse towards a husband yet?

Fres: Faith, Madame, shee has suitors, but they will not suite her, me thinkes. They will not come off lustily it seemes.

Leu. They will not come on lustily, thou wouldst say.

Fres. I meane, Madame, they are not rich enough.

Leu. But I, Fresco, they are not bold enough. Thy Mistresse is of a liuely attractiue blood, Fresco, and in truth she is of my mind for that. A poore spirit is poorer than a poore purse. Giue me a fellow that brings not onely temptation with him, but has the actiuitie of wit and auda-citie of spirit to apply euery word and gesture of a woman's speech and behauiour to his owne desire, and make her beleeue shee's the suitor her selfe. Neuer giue backe till he has made her yeeld to it.

Fres. Indeede among our equals, Madame; but other-wise we shall be put horribly out o' coun-tenance.

Leu. Thou art deceiu'd, Fresco.   Ladyes are as cour-
  teous as Yeomen's wiues, and me thinkes they
  should be more gentle.   Hot diet and soft ease
  makes 'em, like waxe alwaies kept warme,
  more easie to take impression.—Prithee untie
  my shooe.—What, art thou shamefac'd too ?
  Goe roundly to worke, man.   My legge is not
  goutie : 'twill endure the feeling I warrant thee.
  Come hither, Fresco ; thine ear.   S'daintie, I
  mistooke the place, I miss'd thine eare and hit
  thy lip.

Fres. Your Ladiship has made me blush.

Leu. That showes th'art full o' lustie bloud and thou
  knowest not how to use it.   Let mee see thy
  hand.   Thou shouldst not be shamefac'd by thy
  hand, Fresco.   Here's a brawny flesh and a
  hairy skinne, both signes of an able body.   I
  doe not like these flegmaticke, smooth-skinn'd,
  soft-flesh'd fellowes.   They are like candied
  suckets when they begin to perish, which I
  would always emptie my closet of, and giue
  'em my chamber-maid.—I haue some skill in
  Palmestry : by this line that stands directly
  against mee thou shouldst be neare a good for-

tune, Fresco, if thou hadst the grace to entertaine it.

Fres. O what is that, Madame, I pray?

Leu. No lesse then the loue of a faire Lady, if thou dost
not lose her with faint-heartednesse.

Fres. A Lady, Madame? Alas, a Lady is a great thing:
I cannot compasse her.

Leu. No? Why I am a Lady. Am I so great I cannot be compassed? Claspe my waist, and try.

Fres. I could finde i' my heart, Madame—

SEBASTIAN *knockes within.*

Leu. 'Uds body, my Husband! Faint-hearted foole! I
think thou wert begotten betweene the North-
pole and the congeal'd passage. Now, like an
ambitious Coward that betrayes himselfe with
fearefull delay, you must suffer for the treason
you neuer committed. Goe, hide thy selfe behind yond arras instantly.

[FRESCO *hides himselfe*] *Enter* SEBASTIAN.

Sebastian! What doe you here so late?

Seba. Nothing yet, but I hope I shall.—*Kisses her.*

Leu. Y'are very bold.

Seba. And you very valiant, for you met mee at full Carriere.

Leu. You come to ha' me moue your father's reconciliation. I'll write a word or two i' your behalfe.

Seba. A word or two, Madame? That you doe for mee will not be contain'd in lesse then the compasse of two sheetes. But in plaine termes shall wee take the opportunitie of priuatenesse?

Leu. What to doe?

Seba. To dance the beginning of the world after the English manner.

Leu. Why not after the French or Italian?

Seba. Fie! They dance it preposterously; backward!

Leu. Are you so actiue to dance?

Seba. I can shake my heeles.

Leu. Y'are well made for't.

Scba. Measure me from top to toe you shall not finde mee differ much from the true standard of proportion.

BELFOREST *knockes within.*

Leu. I thinke I am accurs'd, Sebastian. There's one at the doore has beaten opportunitie away from us. In briefe, I loue thee, and it shall not be long before I giue thee a testimony of it. To saue thee now from suspition doe no more but draw thy Rapier, chafe thy selfe, and when hee comes in, rush by without taking notice of him. Onely seeme to be angry, and let me alone for the rest.

Enter BELFOREST.

Seba. Now by the hand of Mercurie.

Exit SEBASTIAN.

Bel. What's the matter, Wife?

Leu. Ooh, Ooh, Husband!

Bel. Prithee what ail'st thou, woman?

Leu. O feele my pulse. It beates, I warrant you. Be patient a little, sweete Husband : tarry but till my breath come to me againe and I'll satisfie you.

Bel. What ailes Sebastian? He lookes so distractedly.

Leu. The poore Gentleman's almost out on's wits I
thinke.   You remember the displeasure his
Father tooke against him about the liberty of
speech he us'd euen now, when your daughter
went to be marryed ?

Bel. Yes.   What of that?

Leu. 'T has craz'd him sure.   He met a poore man i'
the street euen now.   Upon what quarrell I know
not, but he pursued him so violently that if
my house had not beene his rescue he had
surely kild him.

Bel. What a strange desperate young man is that !

Leu. Nay, husband, he grew so in rage, when hee saw
the man was conueyed from him, that he was
ready euen to haue drawne his naked weapon
upon mee.   And had not your knocking at
the doore preuented him, surely he'd done
something to mee.

Bel. Where's the man ?

Leu. Alas, here !   I warrant you the poore fearefull
soule is scarce come to himselfe againe yet.—
If the foole haue any wit he will apprehend
mee. [*Aside.*]—Doe you heare, sir ?   You may

be bold to come forth : the Fury that haunted
you is gone.

*F*RESCO *peepes fearefully forth from behinde the Arras.*

Fres. Are you sure hee is gone ?

Bel. Hee's gone, hee's gone I warrant thee.

Fres. I would I were gone too.   H's shooke mee
almost into a dead palsie.

Bel. How fell the difference betweene you ?

Fres. I would I were out at the backe doore.

Bel. Th'art safe enough.   Prithee tell 's the falling out.

Fres. Yes, Sir, when I haue recouered my spirits.   My
memorie is almost frighted from mee.—Oh,
so, so, so !—Why Sir, as I came along the
streete, Sir—this same Gentleman came stum-
bling after mee and trod o' my heele.—I
cryed O.   Doe you cry, sirrah ? saies hee.
Let mee see your heele; if it be not hurt Ile
make you cry for something.   So he claps my
head betweene his legges and pulles off my
shooe.   I hauing shifted no sockes in a sen-
night, the Gentleman cryed foh ! and said my

feete were base and cowardly feete, they stunke
for feare.   Then hee knock'd my shooe about
my pate, and I cryed O once more.   In the
meane time comes a shag-hair'd dogge by, and
rubbes against his shinnes.   The Gentleman
tooke the dog in shagge-haire to be some
Watch-man in a rugge gowne, and swore hee
would hang mee up at the next doore with my
lanthorne in my hand, that passengers might
see their way as they went, without rubbing
against Gentlemen's shinnes.   So, for want of a
Cord, hee tooke his owne garters off, and as
hee was going to make a nooze, I watch'd my
time and ranne away.   And as I ranne, indeed
I bid him hang himselfe in his owne garters.
So hee, in choler, pursued mee hither, as you
see.

Bel. Why, this sauours of distraction.

Leu. Of meere distraction.

Fres. Howsoeuer it sauours I am sure it smels like a lye.
                                                    [*Aside*].

Bel. Thou maist goe forth at the backe doore, honest
    fellow; the way is priuate and safe.

Fres. So it had neede, for your fore-doore here is both
common and dangerous.

Exit BELFOREST.

Leu. Good night, honest Fresco.

Fres. Good night, Madame. If you get mee kissing o'
Ladies againe !—   *Exit* FRESCO.

Leu. This fals out handsomely.
But yet the matter does not well succeed,
Till I haue brought it to the very deede.

Exit.

[SCENE VI.]

Enter CHARLEMONT *in Armes, a* MUSQUETIER, *and a*
SERIEANT.

Charl. Serjeant, what houre o' the night is 't?

Ser. About one.

Charl. I would you would relieue me, for I am
So heauie that I shall ha' much adoe
To stand out my perdu. [*Thunder and Lightning.*

Ser. I'll e'en but walke
The round, Sir, and then presently returne.

Soul. For God's sake, Serjeant, relieue me. Aboue fiue

houres together in so foule a stormy night as
this !

Ser. Why 'tis a musique, Souldier.   Heauen and earth
are now in consort, when the Thunder and the
Canon play one to another.

Exit SERJEANT.

Charl. I know not why I should be thus inclin'd
To sleepe.   I feele my disposition press'd
With a necessitie of heauines.
Souldier, if thou hast any better eyes,
I prithee wake mee when the Serjeant comes.

Soul. Sir, 'tis so darke and stormy that I shall
Scarce either see or heare him, ere hee comes
Upon mee.

Charl. I cannot force my selfe to wake.—   *Sleepes.*

Enter the Ghost of MONTFERRERS.

Mont. Returne to France, for thy old Father's dead,
And thou by murther disinherited.
Attend with patience the successe of things,
But leaue reuenge unto the King of kings.   *Exit*

CHARLEMONT *starts and wakes.*

Charl. O my affrighted soule, what fearefull dreame

Was this that wak'd mee?   Dreames are but the
   rais'd
Impressions of premeditated things
By serious apprehension left upon
Our mindes, or else th' imaginary shapes
Of obiects proper to th' complexion, or
The dispositions of our bodyes.   These
Can neither of them be the cause why I
Should dreame thus ; for my mind has not been
   mou'd
With any one conception of a thought
To such a purpose ; nor my nature wont
To trouble me with phantasies of terror.
It must be something that my Genius would
Informe me of.   Now gratious heauen forbid !
Oh ! let my Spirit be depriu'd of all
Fore-sight and knowledge, ere it understand
That vision acted, or diuine that act
To come.   Why should I thinke so ?   Left I not
My worthy Father i' the kìnd regard
Of a most louing Uncle ?   Souldier, saw'st
No apparition of a man ?

Soul. You dreame,

Sir.   I sawe nothing.

Charl. Tush ! these idle dreames
Are fabulous.   Our boyling phantasies
Like troubled waters falsifie the shapes
Of things retain'd in them, and make 'em seeme
Confounded when they are distinguish'd.   So,
My actions daily conuersant with warre,
The argument of bloud and death had left
Perhaps th' imaginary presence of
Some bloudy accident upon my minde,
Which, mix'd confusedly with other thoughts,
Whereof th' remembrance of my Father might
Be one presented, all together seeme
Incorporate, as if his body were
The owner of that bloud, the subiect of
That death, when hee's at Paris and that bloud
Shed here.   It may be thus.   I would not leaue
The warre, for reputation's sake, upon
An idle apprehension, a vaine dreame.

Enter the Ghost.

Soul. Stand.   Stand I say.   No ?   Why then haue at
thee,

Sir.   If you will not stand, Ile make you fall

[fires.]

Nor stand nor fall ?   Nay then, the Diuel's
damme

Has broke her husband's head, for sure it is
A Spirit.

I shot it through, and yet it will not fall.   *Exit.*

The Ghost approaches CHARLEMONT.

Hee fearefully auoids it.

Char. O pardon me, my doubtfull heart was slow
To credit that which I did feare to know.

Exeunt.

ACTUS TERTII SCENA PRIMA.

Enter the Funerall of MONTFERRERS.

D'amville.

Set downe the Body.   Pay Earth what shee lent.
But shee shall beare a liuing monument
To let succeeding ages truely know
That shee is satisfied what hee did owe,
Both principall and use ; because his worth
Was better at his death then at his birth.

A dead march.   Enter the Funerall of CHARLEMONT
as a Souldier.

D'am. And with his Body place that memorie
Of noble Charlemont his worthie Sonne ;
And giue their Graues the rites that doe belong
To Souldiers.   They were Souldiers both.   The
    Father
Held open warre with Sinne, the Sonne with
    bloud :
This in a warre more gallant, that more good.

The first volley.

D'am. There place their Armes, and here their Epitaphes
  And may these Lines suruiue the last of graues.

The Epitaph of MONTFERRERS.

Here lye the Ashes of that Earth and fire,
  whose heat and fruit did feede and warme the
    poore !
And they (as if they would in sighes expire,
  and into teares dissolue) his death deplore.
Hee did that good freely for goodnesse sake
  unforc'd, for gen'rousnesse he held so deare
That hee fëar'd but him that did him make
  and yet he seru'd him more for loue then feare.
So's life prouided that though he did dye
  A sodaine death, yet dyed not sodainely.

The Epitaph of CHARLEMONT.

His Body lies interr'd within this mould,
Who dyed a young man yet departed old,
And in all strength of youth that Man can haue
Was ready still to drop into his graue.
For ag'd in vertue, with a youthfull eye
He welcom'd it, being still prepar'd to dye
And liuing so, though young depriu'd of breath

He did not suffer an untimely death,
But we may say of his braue bless'd decease
He dyed in warre, and yet hee dyed in peace.

The second volley.

D'am. O might that fire reuiue the ashes of
This Phenix! yet the wonder would not be
So great as he was good, and wondered at
For that.   His liues example was so true
A practique of Religion's Theorie
That her Diuinitie seem'd rather the
Description then th' instruction of his life.
And of his goodnesse was his vertuous Sonne
A worthy imitatour.   So that on
These two Herculean pillars where their armes
Are plac'd there may be writ *Non ultra*.   For
Beyond their liues, as well for youth as age,
Nor young nor old, in merit or in name,
Shall e'er exceede their vertues or their fame.

The third volley.

'Tis done.   Thus faire accomplements make foule
Deedes gratious.   Charlemont, come now when
   th' wilt

I'ue buryed under these two marble stones
Thy liuing hopes, and thy dead father's bones.

Exeunt.

Enter CASTABELLA *mourning to the monument of*
CHARLEMONT.

Casta. O thou that knowest me iustly Charlemont's,
Though in the forc'd possession of another.
Since from thine owne free spirit wee receiue it
That our affections cannot be compel'd
Though our actions may, be not displeas'd if on
The altar of his Tombe I sacrifice
My teares.   They are the iewels of my loue
Dissolued into griefe, and fall upon
His blasted Spring, as Aprill dewe upon
A sweet young blossome shak'd before the time.

Enter CHARLEMONT *with a* SERUANT.

Charl. Goe see my Truncks disposed of.   I'll but walk
A turne or two i' th' Church and follow you.

Exit SERUANT.

O ! here's the fatall monument of my
Dead Father first presented to mine eye.
What's here ?—' *In memory of* Charlemont ?'

Some false relation has abus'd beliefe.

I am deluded.   But I thanke thee, Heauen.

For euer let me be deluded thus.

My Castabella mourning o'er my Hearse?

Sweete Castabella, rise.   I am not dead,

Casta. O heauen defend mee !

Fals in a swoune.

Charl. I—Beshrew my rash

And inconsid'rate passion.—Castabella !

That could not thinke—my Castabella !—that

My sodaine presence might affright her sense.—

I prithee (my affection) pardon mee. [*Shee rises.*]

Reduce thy understanding to thine eye.

Within this habite, which thy misinform'd

Conceipt takes onely for a shape, liue both

The soule and body of thy Charlemont.

Casta. I feele a substance warme, and soft, and moist,

Subiect to the capacitie of sense.

Charl. Which Spirits are not ; for their essence is

Aboue the nature and the order of

Those Elements whereof our senses are

Created.   Touch my lip.   Why turn'st thou from

mee ?

Cast. Griefe aboue griefes ! That which should woe
    releiue

    Wish'd and obtain'd, giues greater cause to grieue.

Charl. Can Castabella thinke it cause of griefe
    That the relation of my death proues false?

Casta. The presence of the person wee affect,
    Being hopelesse to enjoy him, makes our griefe
    More passionate than if wee saw him not.

Charl. Why not enjoy? Has absence chang'd thee?

Casta. Yes.

    From maide to wife.

Charl. Art marryed?

Casta. O ! I am.

Charl. Married?—Had not my mother been a woman
    I should protest against the chastitie
    Of all thy sexe. How can the Marchant or
    The Marriners absent whole yeares from wiues
    Experienc'd in the satisfaction of
    Desire, promise themselues to finde their sheetes
    Unspotted with adultery at their
    Returne, when you that neuer had the sense
    Of actuall temptation could not stay

A few short months ?

Casta. O ! doe but heare me speake.

Charl. But thou wert wise, and didst consider that
A Souldier might be maim'd, and so perhaps
Lose his habilitie to please thee.

Casta. No.
That weaknes pleases me in him I haue.

Char. What, marryed to a man unable too ?
O strange incontinence ! Why, was thy bloud
Increas'd to such a pleurisie of lust,
That of necessitie there must a veyne
Be open'd, though by one that had no skill
To doe 't ?

Casta. Sir, I beseech you heare me.

Charl. Speake.

Casta. Heau'n knowes I am unguiltie of this act.

Charl. Why ?   Wert thou forc'd to doe 't ?

Casta. Heau'n knowes I was.

Charl. What villaine did it ?

Casta. Your Uncle D'amville.
And he that dispossess'd my loue of you

Hath disinherited you of possession.

Charl. Disinherited? wherein haue I deseru'd
  To be depriu'd of my deare Father's loue?

Casta. Both of his loue and him.   His soule's at rest;
  But here your injur'd patience may behold
  The signes of his lamented memorie.

  CHARLEMONT *findes his Father's Monument.*

  H's found it.   When I tooke him for a Ghoast
  I could endure the torment of my feare
  More eas'ly than I can his sorrowes heare.

  Exit.

Charl. Of all men's griefes must mine be singular?
  Without example?   Heere I met my graue.
  And all men's woes are buried i' their graues
  But mine.   In mine my miseries are borne.
  I prithee sorrow leaue a little roome
  In my confounded and tormented mind
  For understanding to deliberate
  The cause or author of this accident.—
  A close aduantage of my absence made
  To dispossesse me both of land and wife,
  And all the profit does arise to him

  6—2

By whom my absence was first mou'd and urg'd.
These circumstances, Uncle, tell me you
Are the suspected author of those wrongs,
Whereof the lightest is more heauie then
The strongest patience can endure to beare.

Exit.

[SCENE II.]

Enter D'AMVILLE, SEBASTIAN, *and* LANGUEBEAU.

D'am. Now, Sir, your businesse?

Sebà. My Annuitie.

D'am. Not a deniere.

Seba. How would you ha' me liue?

D'am. Why turne Cryer.   Cannot you turne Cryer?

Seba. Yes.

D'am. Then doe so : y' haue a good voice for 't.
Y'are excellent at crying of a Rape.

Seba. Sir, I confesse in particular respect to your selfe
I was somewhat forgetfull.   Gen'rall honestie
possess'd me.

D'am. Goe, th'art the base corruption of my bloud ;
  And, like a tetter, grow'st unto my flesh.

Seba. Inflict any punishment upon me. The severitie
  shall not discourage me if it be not shamefull,
  so you'l but put money i' my purse. The want
  of money makes a free spirit more mad than
  the possession does an Usurer.

D'am. Not a farthing.

Seba. Would you ha' me turne purse-taker ? 'Tis the
  next way to doe 't. For want is like the
  Racque : it drawes a man to endanger himselfe
  to the gallowes rather than endure it.

Enter CHARLEMONT. D'AMVILLE *counterfaites to take him
  for a ghoast.*

D'am. What art thou ? Stay — Assist my troubled
  sence—
  My apprehension will distract me—Stay.

  LANGUEBEAU SNUFFE *auoides him fearefully.*

Seba. What art thou ? Speake.

Charl. The spirit of Charlemont.

D'am. O ! stay.   Compose me.   I dissolue.

Lang. No.   'Tis prophane.   Spirits are inuisible.   'Tis
the fiend i' the likenesse of Charlemont.   I will
haue no conuersation with Sathan.

Exit SNUFFE.

Seba. The Spirit of Charlemont ?   I'll try that.
   [*Strikes, and the blow return'd.*]
   'Fore God thou sayest true : th'art all Spirit.
D'am. Goe, call the Officers.

Exit D'AMVILLE.

Charl. Th'art a villaine, and the sonne of a villaine.

Seba. You lye.
   Fight.
   SEBASTIAN *is downe.*

Char. Haue at thee.

Enter the Ghost of MONTFERRERS.

Reuenge, to thee I'll dedicate this worke.

Mont. Hold, Charlemont.
   Let him reuenge my murder and thy wrongs
   To whom the Justice of Reuenge belongs.   *Exit.*

Char. You torture me betweene the passion of
My bloud and the religion of my soule.

SEBASTIAN *rises.*

Seba. A good honest fellow !

Enter D'AMVILLE *with Officers.*

D'am. What, wounded ? Apprehend him. Sir, is this
Your salutation for the courtesie
I did you when wee parted last ? You haue
Forgot I lent you a thousand Crownes. First, let
Him answere for this riot. When the Law
Is satisfied for that, an action for
His debt shall clap him up againe. I tooke
You for a Spirit and Ile conjure you
Before I ha' done.

Charl. No, I'll turne Coniurer. Diuell !
Within this Circle, in the midst of all
Thy force and malice, I coniure thee doe
Thy worst.

D'am. Away with him.

Exeunt Officers with CHARLEMONT.

Seba. Sir, I haue got
  A scratch or two here for your sake.   I hope
  You'll giue mee money to pay the Surgeon.

D'am. Borachio, fetch me a thousand Crownes.   I am
  Content to countenance the freedome of
  Your spirit when 'tis worthily imployed.
  A God's name giue behauiour the full scope
  Of gen'rous libertie, but let it not
  Disperse and spend it selfe in courses of
  Unbounded licence.   Here, pay for your hurts.

  Exit D'AMVILLE.

Seba. I thanke you, sir.—Gen'rous libertie !—that is to
  say, freely to bestow my habilities to honest
  purposes.   Me thinkes I should not follow that
  instruction now, if hauing the meanes to doe an
  honest office for an honest fellow, I should neglect it.   Charlemont lyes in prison for a thousand Crownes.   Honestie tells mee 'twere well
  done to release Charlemont.   But discretion
  sayes I had much a doe to come by this, and
  when this shall be gone I know not where to
  finger any more, especially if I employ it to
  this use, which is like to endanger mee into my

Father's perpetuall displeasure. And then I may
goe hang my selfe, or be forc'd to doe that will
make another saue mee the labour. No matter,
Charlemont, thou gau'st mee my life, and that's
somewhat of a purer earth then gold, fine as it
is. 'Tis no courtesie, I doe thee but thankful-
nesse. I owe it thee, and Ile pay it. Hee
fought brauely, but the Officers drag'd him vil-
lanously. Arrant knaues! for using him so
discourteously; may the sins o' the poore people
be so few that you sha' not be able to spare so
much out o' your gettings as will pay for the
hyre of a lame staru'd hackney to ride to an
execution, but goe a foote to the gallowes and
be hang'd. May elder brothers turne good
husbands, and younger brothers get good wiues,
that there be no neede of debt-bookes nor use
of Serjeants. May there be all peace, but i' the
warre and all charitie, but i' the Diuell, so that
prisons may be turn'd to Hospitals, though the
Officers liue o' the beneuolence. If this curse
might come to passe, the world would say,
Blessed be he that curseth. *Exit.*

[SCENE III.]

Enter CHARLEMONT *in prison.*

Charl. I graunt thee, Heauen, thy goodnesse doth com-
    mand
    Our punishments, but yet no further then
    The measure of our sinnes. How should they else
    Be iust ? Or how should that good purpose of
    Thy Justice take effect by bounding men
    Within the confines of humanitie,
    When our afflictions doe exceede our crimes ?
    Then they doe rather teach the barb'rous world
    Examples that extend her cruelties
    Beyond their owne dimentions, and instruct
    Our actions to be much more barbarous.
    O my afflicted soule ! How torment swells
    Thy apprehension with prophane conceipt,
    Against the sacred justice of my God !
    Our owne constructions are the authors of
    Our miserie. We neuer measure our
    Conditions but with Men aboue us in
    Estate. So while our Spirits labour to
    Be higher then our fortunes, th' are more base.

Since all those attributes which make men seeme
Superiour to us, are Man's subjects and
Were made to serue him.   The repining Man
Is of a seruile spirit to deiect
The value of himselfe below their estimation.

Enter SEBASTIAN *with the Keeper.*

Seba. Here.   Take my sword.—How now, my wilde
Swag'rer?   Y'are tame enough now, are you
not?   The penurie of a prison is like a soft con-
sumption.   'Twill humble the pride o' your
mortalitie, and arme your soule in compleate
patience to endure the weight of affliction without feeling it.   What, hast no musicke in thee?
Th' hast trebles and bases enough.   Treble
injurie and base usage.   But trebles and bases
make Poore musick without meanes.   Thou
want'st Meanes, dost?   What?   Dost droope?
art deiected?

Charl. No, Sir.   I haue a heart aboue the reach
Of thy most violent maliciousnesse;
A fortitude in scorne of thy contempt
(Since Fate is pleas'd to haue me suffer it)

That can beare more then thou has power t' inflict.
I was a Baron.   That thy Father has
Depriu'd me of.   In stead of that I am
Created King.   I'ue lost a Signiorie
That was confin'd within a piece of earth,
A Wart upon the body of the world,
But now I am an Emp'rour of a world,
This little world of Man.   My passions are
My Subiects, and I can command them laugh,
Whilst thou dost tickle 'em to death with miserie.

Seba.   'Tis brauely spoken and I loue thee for 't.   Thou
liest here for a thousand crownes.   Here are a
thousand to redeeme thee.   Not for the ran-
some o' my life thou gau'st mee,—That I value
not at one crowne—'Tis none o' my deed.
Thanke my Father for 't.   'Tis his goodnesse.
Yet hee lookes not for thankes.   For he does it
under hand, out of a reseru'd disposition to doe
thee good without ostentation.—Out o' great
heart you'l refuse 't now ; will you ?

Charl. No.   Since I must submit my selfe to Fate
I neuer will neglect the offer of
One benefit, but entertaine them as

Her fauours and th' inductions to some end
Of better fortune.   As whose instrument,
I thanke thy courtesie.

Seba. Well, come along.   *Exeunt.*

[SCENE IV.]

Enter D'AMVILLE *and* CASTABELLA.

D'am. Daughter, you doe not well to urge me.   I
Ha' done no more then Justice.   Charlemont
Shall die and rot in prison, and 'tis iust.

Casta. O Father, Mercie is an attribute
As high as Justice, an essentiall part
Of his unbounded goodnesse, whose diuine
Impression, forme, and image man should beare !
And, me thinks, Man should loue to imitate
His Mercie, since the onely countenance
Of Justice were destruction, if the sweet
And louing fauour of his mercie did
Not mediate betweene it and our weaknesse.

D'am. Forbeare.   You will displease me.   He shall rot.

Casta. Deare Sir, since by your greatnesse you
Are nearer heau'n in place, be nearer it

In goodnesse. Rich men should transcend the
  poore
As clouds the Earth, rais'd by the comfort of
The Sunne to water dry and barren grounds.
If neither the impression in your soule
Of goodnesse, nor the dutie of your place
As goodnesse substitute can moue you, then
Let nature which in Sauages, in beasts
Can stirre to pittie, tell you that hee is
Your kinsman.—

D'am. You expose your honestie
To strange construction.   Why should you so
  urge
Release for Charlemont ?   Come, you professe
More nearenesse to him then your modestie
Can answere.   You haue tempted my suspition.
I tell thee hee shall starue, and dye, and rot.

Enter CHARLEMONT *and* SEBASTIAN.

Charl. Uncle, I thanke you.

D'am. Much good do it you.—Who did release him ?

Seba. I.   *Exit* CASTABELLA.

D'am. You are a villaine.

Seba. Y'are my Father.   *Exit* SEBASTIAN.

D'am. I must temporize.—   [Aside]
　　　Nephew, had not his open freedome made
　　　My disposition knowne, I would ha' borne
　　　The course and inclination of my loue
　　　According to the motion of the Sunne,
　　　Inuisibly injoyed and understood.

Charl. That showes your good works are directed to
　　　No other end then goodnesse.   I was rash,
　　　I must confesse.   But—

D'am. I will excuse you.
　　　To lose a Father and, as you may thinke,
　　　Be disinherited, it must be graunted
　　　Are motiues to impatience.   But for death,
　　　Who can auoide it?   And for his estate
　　　In the uncertaintie of both your liues
　　　'Twas done discreetly to confer 't upon
　　　A knowne Successour being the next in bloud.
　　　And one, deare Nephew, whom in time to come
　　　You shall haue cause to thanke.   I will not be
　　　Your dispossessour but your Gardian.
　　　I will supply your Father's vacant place
　　　To guide your greene improuidence of youth,

And make you ripe for your inheritance.

Charl. Sir, I embrace your gen'rous promises.

Enter ROUSARD *sicke and* CASTABELLA.

Rousa. Embracing! I behold the obiect that
　　　Mine eye affects.　Deere Cosin Charlemont.

D'am. My elder Sonne!　He meetes you happily.
　　　For with the hand of our whole family
　　　We enterchange th' indenture of our Loues.

Charl. And I accept it.　Yet not so ioyfully
　　　Because y'are sicke.

D'am. Sir, his affection's sound
　　　Though hee be sicke in body.

Rousa. Sicke indeede.
　　　A gen'rall weakenesse did surprise my health
　　　The very day I married Castabella
　　　As if my sicknesse were a punishment
　　　That did arrest me for some iniurie
　　　I then committed.　Credit me, my Loue,
　　　I pittie thy ill fortune to be match'd
　　　With such a weake, unpleasing bedfellow.

Casta. Beleeue me, Sir, it neuer troubles me.
　　　I am as much respectlesse to enioy

Such pleasure, as ignorant what it is.

Charl. Thy Sexe's wonder.   Unhappy Charlemont!

D'am. Come, let's to supper.   There we will confirme
The eternall bond of our concluded loue.

Exeunt.

ACTUS QUARTI SCENA PRIMA.

Enter CATAPLASMA *and* SOQUETTE *with Needle-worke.*

Cataplasma.

Come, Soquette, your worke! let's examine your
worke.   What's here? a Medlar with a Plum-
tree growing hard by it; the leaues o' the Plum-
tree falling off; the gumme issuing out o' the
perish'd joynts; and the branches some of 'em
dead, and some rotten; and yet but a young
Plum-tree.   In good sooth very prettie.

Soqu. The Plum-tree, forsooth, growes so neare the
Medlar that the Medlar suckes and drawes all
the sap from it and the natural strength o' the
ground, so that it cannot prosper.

Cata. How conceipted you are ! But heere th'ast made
a tree to beare no fruit.   Why's that ?

Soqu. There growes a Sauin-tree next it, forsooth.

Cata. Forsooth you are a little too wittie in that.

Enter SEBASTIAN.

Seba. But this Honisuckle windes about this white-
thorne very prettily and louingly, sweet Mistresse Cataplasma.

Cata. Monsieur Sebastian ! in good sooth very uprightly
welcome this euening.

Seba. What, moralizing upon this Gentlewoman's needle-
worke ?   Let's see.

Cata. No, sir.   Onely examining whether it be done to
the true nature and life o' the thing.

Seba. Heere y' haue set a Medlar with a Batcheler's button o' one side and a snaile o' th' tother.   The
Batcheler's button should haue held his head
up more pertly towards the Medlar : the snaile
o' th' tother side should ha' beene wrought with
an artificiall lazinesse, doubling his taile and
putting out his horne but halfe the length.   And

then the Medlar falling (as it were) from the lazie Snaile and ending towards the pert Batcheler's button, their branches spreading and winding one within another as if they did embrace. But heere's a morall. A poppring Peare-tree growing upon the banke of a Riuer seeming continually to looke downewards into the water as if it were enamour'd of it, and euer as the fruit ripens lets it fall for loue (as it were) into her lap. Which the wanton Streame, like a Strumpet, no sooner receiues but she carries it away and bestowes it upon some other creature she maintaines, still seeming to play and dally under the Poppring so long that it has almost wash'd away the earth from the roote, and now the poore Tree stands as if it were readie to fall and perish by that whereon it spent all the substance it had.

Cata. Morall for you that loue those wanton running waters.

Seba. But is not my Lady Leuidulcia come yet?

Cata. Her purpose promis'd us her companie ere this. Sirrie, your Lute and your Booke.

Seba. Well said.   A lesson o' th' Lute, to entertaine the time with till she comes.

Cata. Sol, fa, mi, la. —— Mi, mi, mi. —— Precious! Dost not see *mi* betweene the two Crotchets? Strike mee full there. —— So —— forward. This is a sweet straine, and thou finger'st it beastly. *Mi* is a laerg there, and the prick that stands before *mi* a long; alwaies halfe your note. —— Now —— Runne your diuision pleasingly with these quavers.   Obserue all your graces i' the touch. —— Heere's a sweet cloze —— strike it full; it sets off your musicke delicately.

Enter LANGUEBEAU SNUFFE *and* LEUIDULCIA.

Lang. Puritie be in this House.

Cata. 'Tis now enter'd; and welcome with your good Ladiship.

Seba. Cease that musicke.   Here's a sweeter instrument.

Leuid. Restraine your libertie.   See you not Snuffe?

Seba. What does the Stinkard here? put Snuffe out. He's offensiue.

Leuid. No. The credit of his companie defends my
being abroad from the eye of Suspition.

Cata. Wilt please your Ladyship goe up into the Closet?
There are those Falles and Tyres I tolde you of.

Leuid. Monsieur Snuffe, I shall request your patience.
My stay will not be long. —[*Exit cum Sebast.*]

Lang. My duty, Madame. —— Falles and Tyres! I
begin to suspect what Falles and Tyres you
meane. My Lady and Sebastian the Falle and
the Tyre, and I the shadow. I perceiue the
puritie of my conuersation is us'd but for a propertie to couer the uncleanenesse of their purposes. The very contemplation o' the thing
makes the spirit of the flesh begin to wriggle in
my bloud. And heere my desire has met with
an object alreadie. This Gentlewoman, me
thinkes, should be swayed with the motion,
liuing in a house where mouing example is so
common. —— Mistresse Cataplasma, my Lady,
it seemes, has some businesse that requires her
stay. The fairnesse o' the euening inuites me
into the ayre. Will it please you giue this
Gentlewoman leaue to leaue her worke and

walk a turne or two with me for honest recreation?

Cata. With all my heart, Sir. Goe, Soquette : giue ear
to his instructions. You may get understanding
by his companie, I can tell you.

Lang. In the way of holinesse, Mistresse Cataplasma.

Cata. Good Monsieur Snuffe! —— I will attend your
returne.

Lang. Your hand, Gentlewoman.—
The flesh is humble till the Spirit moue it.
But when 'tis rais'd it will command aboue it.

Exeunt.

[SCENE II.]

Enter D'AMVILLE, CHARLEMONT, *and* BORACHIO.

D'am. Your sadnesse and the sicknesse of my Sonne
Haue made our company and conference
Lesse free and pleasing then I purpos'd it.

Char. Sir, for the present I am much unfit
For conuersation or societie.
With pardon I will rudely take my leaue.

D'am. Good night, deere Nephew.   *Exit Charlemont.*
Seest thou that same man?

Bora. Your meaning, Sir?

D'am. That fellowe's life, Borachio,
Like a superfluous Letter in the Law,
Endangers our assurance.

Bora. Scrape him out.

D'am. Wilt doe 't?

Bora. Giue me your purpose—I will doe 't.

D'am. Sad melancholy has drawne Charlemont
With meditation on his Father's death
Into the solitarie walke behind the Church.

Bora. The Churchyard? 'Tis the fittest place for death.
Perhaps he's praying. Then he's fit to die.
We'll send him charitably to his graue.

D'am. No matter how thou tak'st him. First take this.—

Gives him a Pistole.

Thou knowest the place. Obserue his passages
And with the most aduantage make a stand,
That, fauour'd by the darknesse of the night,
His brest may fall upon thee at so neare
A distance that he sha' not shunne the blow.
The deede once done, thou mai'st retire with safety.

The place is unfrequented, and his death
Will be imputed to th' attempt of theeues.

Bor. Be carelesse.   Let your mind be free and cleare.
This Pistoll shall discharge you of your feare.

Exit.

D'am. But let me call my projects to accompt
For what effect and end have I engag'd
My selfe in all this bloud ?   To leaue a state
To the succession of my proper bloud.
But how shall that succession be continued ?
Not in my elder Sonne, I feare.   Disease
And weaknesse haue disabled him for issue.
For th' other,—his loose humour will endure
No bond of marriage.   And I doubt his life,
His spirit is so boldly dangerous.
O pittie that the profitable end
Of such a prosp'rous murder should be lost !
Nature forbid !   I hope I haue a body
That will not suffer me to loose my labour
For want of issue yet.   But then 't must be
A Bastard.—Tush ! they onely father bastards
That father other men's begettings.   Daughter !

Be it mine oune.   Let it come whence it will
I am resolu'd.   Daughter !

Enter Servant.

Seru. My Lord.

D'am. I prithee call my Daughter.

—Enter CASTA.

Casta. Your pleasure, Sir.

D'am. Is thy Husband i' bed ?

Casta. Yes, my Lord.

D'am. The euening's faire. I prithee walke a turne or two.

Casta. Come, Jaspar.

D'am. No.

Wee'l walke but to the corner o' the Church ;
And I haue something to speake priuately.

Casta. No matter ; stay.   *—Exit Seruant.*

D'am. This falles out happily.   *—Exeunt.*

[SCENE III.]

THE CHURCHYARD.

Enter CHARLEMONT,—BORACHIO *dogging him in the
Churchyard.   The Clocke strikes twelue.*

Charl. Twelue.

   Bor. 'Tis a good houre : 'twill strike one anon.

Charl. How fit a place for contemplation is this dead of
        night, among the dwellings of the dead.—This
        graue.—Perhaps th' inhabitant was in his life
        time the possessour of his oune desires.   Yet
        in the midd'st of all his greatnesse and his
        wealth he was lesse rich and lesse contented
        then in this poore piece of earth lower and
        lesser then a Cottage.   For heere he neither
        wants, nor cares.   Now that his body sauours
        of corruption
H' enioyes a sweeter rest then e'er hee did
Amongst the sweetest pleasures of this life
For heere there's nothing troubles him.—And there
—In that graue lies another.   He, perhaps,
Was in his life as full of miserie

As this of happinesse.   And here's an end
Of both.   Now both their states are equall.   O
That man with so much labour should aspire
To worldly height, when in the humble earth
The world's condition's at the best, or scorne
Inferiour men since to be lower than
A worme is to be higher then a King.

Bora. Then fall and rise.

       [*Discharges the pistol.   Giues false fire.*]

Charl. What villaines hand was that ?
    Saue thee, or thou shalt perish.

           (*They fight.*)

Bora. Zownes ! unsau'd
    I thinke.   —[*Falls.*]

Charl. What ?   Haue I kill'd him ?   Whatsoe'er thou
    beest
    I would thy hand had prosper'd.   For I was
    Unfit to liue and well prepar'd to die.
    What shall I doe ?   Accuse my selfe ?   Submit
    Me to the law ?   And that will quickly end
    This violent encrease of miserie.
    But 'tis a murther to be accessarie

To mine owne death.   I will not.   I will take
This opportunitie to scape.   It may
Be Heau'n reserues me to some better end.

Exit CHARLEMONT.

Enter SNUFFE *and* SOQUETTE *into the Churchyard.*

Soqu. Nay, good Sir, I dare not.   In good sooth I
come of a generation both by Father and
Mother that were all as fruitfull as Costard-
mongers' wiues.

Snu. Tush then a Timpanie is the greatest danger can
be fear'd.   Their fruitfulnesse turnes but to a
certaine kind of flegmatique windie disease.

Soqu. I must put my understanding to your trust, Sir.
I would be loath to be deceiu'd.

Snu. No, conceiue thou sha't not.   Yet thou shalt
profit by my instruction too.   My bodie is not
euery day drawne dry, wench.

Soqu. Yet mee thinkes, Sir, your want of use should
rather make your body like a Well,—the lesser
'tis drawne, the sooner it growes dry.

Snu. Thou shalt try that instantly.

Soqu. But we want place and opportunity.

Snu. We haue both.   This is the backe side of the
House which the superstitious call Saint Winifred's Church, and is verily a conuenient unfrequented place.—

Where under the close Curtaines of the night—

Soqu. You purpose i' the darke to make me light.

(SNUFFE *Pulles out a sheete, a haire, and a beard.*)

But what ha' you there ?

Snu. This disguise is for securitie's sake, wench.
There's a talke, thou know'st, that the Ghoast
of olde Montferrers walks.   In this Church he
was buried.   Now if any stranger fall upon us
before our businesse be ended, in this disguise
I shall be taken for that Ghoast, and neuer be
call'd to examination, I warrant thee.   Thus
wee shall scape both preuention and discouerie.
How doe I looke in this habite, wench ?

Soq. So like a Ghoast that notwithstanding I haue
some foreknowledge of you, you make my haire
stand almost on end.

Snu. I will try how I can kisse in this beard.—O fie,

fie, fie I will put it off and then kisse, and
then put it on. I can doe the rest without
kissing.

Enter CHARLEMONT *doubtfully with his sword drawne;*
is upon them before they are aware. They runne out
diuers waies, and leaue the disguise.

Charl. What ha' wee heere? a Sheete! a haire! a beard!
What end was this disguise intended for?
No matter what. I'le not expostulate
The purpose of a friendly accident.
Perhaps it may accommodate my 'scape.
——I feare I am pursued. For more assurance.
I'le hide me heere i' th' Charnell house,
This convocation-house of dead men's sculles.

[*To get into the Charnell house he takes holde of a Death's*
head; it slips and staggers him.]

Death's head, deceiu'st my hold?
Such is the trust to all mortalitie.

[*Hides himselfe in the Charnell house.*]

Enter D'AMVILLE *and* CASTABELLA.

Casta. My Lord, the night growes late.   Your Lordship
    spake
    Of something you desir'd to moue in priuate.

D'am. Yes.   Now Ile speake it.   Th' argument is loue.
    The smallest ornament of thy sweet forme
    (That abstract of all pleasure) can command
    The sences into passion and thy entire
    Perfection is my obiect, yet I loue thee
    With the freedome of my reason.   I can giue
    Thee reason for my loue.

Casta. Loue me, my Lord ?
    I doe beleeue it, for I am the wife
    Of him you loue.

D'am. 'Tis true.   By my perswasion thou wert forc'd
    To marrie one unable to performe
    The office of a Husband.   I was author
    Of the wrong.
    My conscience suffers under 't, and I would
    Disburthen it by satisfaction.

Casta. How ?

D'am. I will supply that pleasure to thee which he cannot.

Casta. Are y' a diuell or a man?

D'am. A man, and such a man as can returne
Thy entertainment with as prodigall
A body as the couetous desire,
Or woman euer was delighted with.
So that, besides the full performance of
Thy empty Husband's dutie, thou shalt haue
The joy of children to continue the
Succession of thy bloud.   For the appetite
That steales her pleasure drawes the forces of
The body to an united strength and puts 'em
Altogether into action, neuer failes
Of procreation.   All the purposes
Of man aime but at one of these two ends
Pleasure or profit ; and in this one sweet
Coniunction of our loues they both will meete.
Would it not grieue thee that a Stranger to
Thy bloud should lay the first foundation of
His house upon the ruines of thy family?

Casta. Now Heau'n defend me !   May my memorie
Be utterly extinguish'd, and the heire

Of him that was my Father's enemie
Raise his eternall monument upon
Our ruines, ere the greatest pleasure or
The greatest profit euer tempt me to
Continue it by incest.

D'am. Incest ? Tush !
These distances affinitie obserues
Are articles of bondage cast upon
Our freedomes by our owne objections.
Nature allowes a gen'rall libertie
Of generation to all creatures else.
Shall man
To whose command and use all creatures were
Made subject be lesse free then they ?

Casta O God !
Is Thy unlimited and infinite
Omnipotence lesse free because thou doest
No ill ?
Or if you argue meerely out of nature
Doe you not degenerate from that, and are
You not unworthie the prerogatiue
Of Nature's Maisterpiece, when basely you
Prescribe your selfe authoritie and law

From their examples whom you should command?
I could confute you, but the horror of
The argument confutes my understanding.—
Sir, I know you do but try me in
Your Sonne's behalfe, suspecting that
My strength
And youth of bloud cannot containe themselues
With impotence.——Beleeue me, Sir,
I neuer wrong'd him.   If it be your lust,
O quench it on their prostituted flesh
Whose trade of sinne can please desire with more
Delight and lesse offence.——The poyson o' your
    breath,
Euaporated from so foule a soule,
Infects the ayre more than the dampes that rise
From bodies but halfe rotten in their graues.

D'am. Kisse me.   I warrant thee my breath is sweet.
These dead men's bones lie heere of purpose to
Inuite us to supply the number of
The liuing.   Come, we'l get young bones, and doe't.
I will enioy thee.   No ?   Nay then inuoke
Your great suppos'd protectour ; I will doe't.

Casta. Suppos'd protectour !   Are y' an Atheist ?   Then

I know my prayers and teares are spent in vaine.
O patient Heau'n ! Why dost thou not expresse
Thy wrath in thunder-bolts to teare the frame
Of man in pieces ? How can earth endure
The burthen of this wickednesse without
An earthquake ? Or the angry face of Heau'n
Be not enflam'd with lightning ?

D'am. Coniure up
The Diuell and his Dam : crie to the graues :
The dead can heare thee : inuocate their help.

Casta. O would this Graue might open and my body
Were bound to the dead carkasse of a man
For euer, ere it entertaine the lust
Of this detested villaine !

D'am. Tereus-like
Thus I will force my passage to——

Charl. The Diuell.

[CHARLEMONT *rises in the disguise, and frights* D'AMVILLE
away.]

Now, Lady, with the hand of Charlemont
I thus redeeme you from the arme of lust.
——My Castabella !

8—2

Casta. My deare Charlemont !

Charl. For all my wrongs I thanke thee, gracious Heau'n,
Th'ast made me satisfaction to reserue
Me for this blessed purpose.   Now, sweet Death,
I'le bid thee welcome.   Come, Ile guide thee home,
And then Ile caste my selfe into the armes
Of apprehension, that the law may make
This worthie worke the crowne of all my actions,
Being the best and last.

Casta. The last ?   The law ?
Now Heau'n forbid !   What ha' you done ?

Charl. Why, I have
Kill'd a man ; not murder'd him, my Castabella.
He would ha' murder'd me.

Casta. Then Charlemont
The hand of Heau'n directed thy defence.
That wicked Atheist !   I suspect his plot.

Charl. My life he seekes.   I would he had it since
He has depriu'd mee of those blessings that
Should make mee loue it.   Come, Ile giue it him.

Casta. You sha' not.   I will first expose my selfe

To certaine danger than for my defence
Destroy the man that sau'd mee from destruction.

Charl. Thou canst not satisfie me better than
To be the instrument of my release
From miserie.

Casta. Then worke it by escape.
Leaue mee to this protection that still guards
The innocent.   Or I will be a partner
In your destinie.

Charl. My soule is heauie.   Come, lie downe to rest ;
These are the pillowes whereon men sleepe best.

[*They lie downe with either of them a Death's head for a
pillow.*]

Enter SNUFFE *seeking* SOQUETTE.

Snu. Soquette, Soquette, Soquette !   O art thou there ?
[*He mistakes the body of* BORACHIO *for* SOQUETTE.]

Verily thou lyest in a fine premeditated readinesse
for the purpose.   Come kisse me, sweet
Soquette.—Now puritie defend me from the
Sinne of Sodom.—This is a creature of the mas-

culine gender.—Verily the Man is blasted.—
Yea, cold and stiffe !—Murder, murder, murder;

Exit.

Enter D'AMVILLE *distractedly : starts at the sight of a
Death's head.*

D'am. Why dost thou stare upon me ?   Thou art not
The soull of him I murder'd.   What hast thou
To doe to vexe my conscience ?   Sure thou wert
The head of a most dogged Usurer,
Th'art so uncharitable.   And that Bawde
The skie there : she could shut the windowes and
The dores of this great chamber of the world,
And draw the curtaines of the clouds betweene
Those lights and me, above this bed of Earth
When that same Strumpet Murder and my selfe
Committed sin together.   Then she could
Leaue us i' the darke till the close deed was done.
But now that I begin to feele the loathsome
horrour of my sinne, and, like a Leacher emptied
of his lust, desire to burie my face under my eye-
browes, and would steale from my shame un-
seene, she meetes me

I' the face with all her light corrupted eyes
To challenge payment o' mee.—O beholde !
Yonder's the Ghoast of olde Montferrers, in
A long white sheete climbing yon loftie mountaine
To complaine to Heau'n of me.—
Montferrers ! pox o' fearefulnesse ! Tis nothing
But a faire white cloude. Why, was I borne a
    coward ?
He lies that sayes so. Yet the count'nance of
A bloudlesse worme might ha' the courage now
To turne my bloud to water.
The trembling motion of an Aspen leafe
Would make me like the shadow of that leafe,
Lie shaking under 't. I could now commit
A murder were it but to drinke the fresh
Warme bloud of him I murder'd to supply
The want and weakenesse o' mine owne,
'Tis growne so colde and flegmaticke.

Lang. Murder, murder, murder ! [*Within*]

D'am. Mountaines o'erwhelme mee : the Ghoast of olde
    Montferrers haunts me.

Lang. Murder, murder, murder !

D'am. O were my body circumuolu'd

Within that cloude, that when the thunder teares
His passage open, it might scatter me
To nothing in the ayre !

Enter Languebeau Snuffe *with the Watch.*

Lang. Here you shall finde
The murder'd body.

D'am. Black Beelzebub,
And all his hell-hounds, come to apprehend me ?

Lang. No, my good Lord, wee come to apprehend
The murderer.

D'am. The Ghoast (great Pluto !) was
A foole unfit to be employèd in
Any serious businesse for the state of hell.
Why could not he ha' suffer'd me to raise
The mountaines o' my sinnes with one as damnable
As all the rest, and then ha' tumbled me
To ruine ?   But apprehend me e'en betweene
The purpose and the act before it was
Committed !

Watch. Is this the murderer?   He speakes suspitiously.

Lang. No verily. This is my Lord D'amville. And his distraction, I thinke, growes out of his griefe for the losse of a faithfull seruant. For surely I take him to be Borachio that is slaine.

D'am. Hah! Borachio slaine? Thou look'st like Snuffe, dost not?

Lang. Yes, in sincerity, my Lord.

D'am. Harke thee?—Sawest thou not a Ghoast?

Lang. A Ghoast? Where, my Lord?—I smell a Foxe.

D'am. Heere i' the Churchyard.

Lang. Tush! tush! their walking Spirits are meere imaginarie fables. There's no such thing *in rerum naturo.* Heere is a man slaine. And with the Spirit of consideration I rather think him to be the murderer got into that disguise then any such phantastique toy.

D'am. My braines begin to put themselves in order. I apprehend thee now.—'Tis e'en so.—Borachio, I will search the Center, but Ile finde the murderer.

Watch. Heere, heere, heere.

D'am. Stay.   Asleepe? so soundly
So sweetly upon Death's Heads? and in a place
So full of feare and horrour?   Sure there is
Some other happinesse within the freedome
Of the conscience then my knowledge e'er at-
tain'd to.—Ho, ho, ho !

Charl. Y'are welcome, Uncle.   Had you sooner come
You had beene sooner welcome.   I'm the Man
You seeke.   You sha' not neede examine me.

D'am. My Nephew and my Daughter !   O my deare
Lamented bloud, what Fate has cast you thus
Unhappily upon this accident ?

Charl. You know, Sir, she's as cleare as Chastitie.

D'am. As her owne chastitie.   The time, the place,
All circumstances argue that uncleare.

Casta. Sir, I confesse it ; and repentantly
Will undergoe the selfe same punishment
That Justice shall inflict on Charlemont.

Charl. Unjustly she betrayes her innocence.

Watch. But, Sir, she's taken with you and she must
To prison with you.

D'am. There's no remedie.

Yet were it not my Sonnes bed she abus'd
My land should flie, but both should be excus'd.

Exeunt.

[SCENE IV]

Enter BELFOREST *and a* SERUANT.

Belfo. Is not my wife come in yet ?

Seru. No, my Lord.

Belfo. Me thinkes she's very affectedly enclin'd
To young Sebastian's company o' late.
But jealousie is such a torment that
I am afraid to entertaine it.   Yet
The more I shunne by circumstances to meete
Directly with it, the more ground I finde
To circumuent my apprehension.   First,
I know sh'as a perpetuall appetite,
Which being so oft encounter'd with a man
Of such a bold luxurious freedome as
Sebastian is, and of so promising
A body, her owne bloud corrupted will
Betray her to temptation.

Enter FRESCO *closely.*

Fres. Precious ! I was sent by his Lady to see if her

Lord were in bed. I should ha' done't slily without discouery, and now I am blurted upon 'em before I was aware.   *Exit.*

Belfo. Know not you the Gentlewoman my wife brought home?

Seru. By sight, my Lord. Her man was here but now.

Belfo. Her man? I, prithee, runne and call him quickly. This villaine! I suspect him euer since I found him hid behind the Tapestry. —— Fresco! th'art welcome, Fresco. —— Leaue us. Dost heare, Fresco? Is not my wife at thy Mistresse's?

Fresco. I know not, my Lord.

Belfo. I prithee tell me, Fresco —— we are priuate—— tell me:

Is not thy Mistresse a good wench·?

Fres. How means your Lordship that? A wench o' the trade?

Belfo. Yes faith, Fresco; e'en a wench o' the trade.

Fres. Oh no, my Lord. Those falling diseases cause baldnesse, and my Mistresse recouers the losse of haire, for she is a Periwig-maker.

Belfo. And nothing else?

Fres. Sels Falls and Tyres and Bodies for Ladies, or so.

Belfo. So, Sir ; and she helpes my Lady to falles and
bodies now and then, does she not ?

Fres. At her Ladiship's pleasure, my Lord.

Belfo. Her pleasure, you Rogue ? You are the Pandar
to her pleasure, you Varlet, are you not ? You
know the conueyances betweene Sebastian and
my wife ? Tell me the truth, or by this hand
I'll naile thy bosome to the earth. Stirre not
you Dogge, but quickly tell the truth.

Fres. O yes !   [*Speakes like a Crier.*

Belfo. Is not thy Mistresse a Bawde to my wife ?

Fres. O yes !

Belfo. And acquainted with her trickes, and her plots,
and her deuises ?

Fresco. O yes ! If any man, 'o Court, Citie, or Countrey,
has found my Lady Leuidulcia in bed but my
Lord Belforest, it is Sebastian.

Belfo. What dost thou proclaime it ? Dost thou crie it,
thou villaine ?

Fresco. Can you laugh it, my Lord ? I thought you meant
to proclaime yourselfe cuckold.

Enter the Watch.

Belfo. The Watch met with my wish.   I must request
th' assistance of your offices.

Fresco *runnes away.*

'Sdeath, stay that villaine : pursue him !   *Exeunt.*

[SCENE. V.]

Enter SNUFFE *importuning* SOQUETTE.

Soqu. Nay, if you get me any more into the Churchyard!

Snu. Why, Soquette, I neuer got thee there yet.

Soqu. Got me there !   No, not with childe.

Snu. I promis'd thee I would not, and I was as good
as my word.

Soqu. Yet your word was better then than your deede.
But steale up into the little matted chamber o'
the left hand.

Snu. I prithee let it be the right hand.   Thou *left'st*
me before and I did not like that.

Soqu. Precious quickly —— So soone as my Mistresse
shall be in bed I'll come to you.

Exit Snuffe.

Enter Sebastian, Leuidulcia, *and* Cataplasma.

Cata. I wonder Fresco stayes so long.

Seba. Mistresse Soquet, a word with you.   [*Whispers.*

Leu. If he brings word my Husband is i' bed
    I will aduenture one night's liberty
    To be abroad. ——
    My strange affection to this man ! —— 'Tis like
    That naturall sympathie which e'en among
    The sencelesse creatures of the earth commands
    A mutuall inclination and consent.
    For though it seemes to be the free effect
    Of mine owne voluntarie loue, yet I can
    Neither restraine it nor giue reason for 't.
    But now 'tis done, and in your power it lies
    To saue my honour, or dishonour me.

Cata. Enioy your pleasure, Madame, without feare.
    I neuer will betray the trust you haue
    Committed to me.   And you wrong your selfe
    To let consideration of the sinne
    Molest your conscience.   Me thinkes 'tis unjust
    That a reproach should be inflicted on
    A woman for offending but with one,

When 'tis a light offence in Husbands to
Commit with many.

Leui. So it seemes to me.——

Why, how now, Sebastian, making loue to that
Gentlewoman ?   How many mistresses ha' you
i' faith ?

Seba. In faith, none ; for I think none of 'em are faithfull ; but otherwise, as many as cleane shirts.
The loue of a woman is like a mushroom,—it
growes in one night and will serue somewhat
pleasingly next morning to breakfast, but afterwards waxes fulsome and unwholesome.

Cata. Nay, by Saint Winifred, a woman's loue lasts as
long as winter fruit.

Seba. 'Tis true—till new come in.   By my experience
no longer.

Enter FRESCO *running.*

Fresco. Some bodie's doing has undone us, and we are
like to pay dearely for't.

Sebast. Pay deare ?   For what ?

Fresco. Wil't not be a chargeable reckoning, thinke you,
when heere are halfe a dozen fellowes comming

to call us to accompt, with eu'rie man a seuerall
bill in his hand that wee are not able to discharge.   *[Knocke at the doore.*

Cata. Passion o' me !   What bouncing's that ?
    Madame withdraw your selfe.

Leuid. Sebastian, if you loue me, saue my honour.
                                Exeunt.

Seba. What violence is this ?   What seeke you ?   Zownes !
    You shall not passe.

       Enter BELFOREST *and the Watch.*

Belfo. Pursue the Strumpet.   Villaine, giue mee way
    Or I will make my passage through thy bloud.

Seba. My bloud will make it slipperie, my Lord,
    'Twere better you would take another way.
    You may hap fall else.

  *[They fight.   Both slaine. * SEBASTIAN *falles first.]*

Seba. I ha't i' faith.   *Dies.*

  While BELFOREST *is staggering enter* LEUIDULCIA.

Leuid. O God ! my Husband ! my Sebastian ! Husband !
    Neither can speake, yet both report my shame.
    Is this the sauing of my Honour when
    Their bloud runnes out in riuers, and my lust

The fountaine whence it flowes? Deare Hus-
  band, let
Not thy departed spirit be displeas'd
If with adult'rate lips I kisse thy cheeke.
Heere I behold the hatefulnesse of lust
Which brings me kneeling to embrace him dead
Whose body liuing I did loathe to touch.
Now I can weepe.   But what can teares doe good
When I weepe onely water, they weepe bloud.
But could I make an Ocean with my teares
That on the floud this broken vessell of
My body, laden heauie with light lust,
Might suffer shipwrack and so drowne my shame.
Then weeping were to purpose, but alas!
The Sea wants water enough to wash away
The foulenesse of my name.   O! in their wounds
I feele my honour wounded to the death.
Shall I out-liue my Honour?   Must my life
Be made the world's example?   Since it must
Then thus in detestation of my deede
To make th' example moue more forceably
To vertue thus I seale it with a death
As full of horrour as my life of sinne.

                        Stabs her selfe.

Enter the Watch with CATAPLASMA, FRESCO, SNUFFE,
and SOQUETTE.

Watch. Hold, Madame !   Lord, what a strange night is
this !

Snu. May not Snuffe be suffer'd to goe out of himselfe?

Watch. Nor you, nor any.   All must goe with us.
O with what vertue lust should be withstood !
Since 'tis a fire quench'd seldome without bloud.

Exeunt.

ACTUS QUINTI SCENA PRIMA.

*Musicke. A clozet discouer'd. A Seruant sleeping with
lights and money before him.*

Enter D'AMVILLE.

D'amville.

What, sleep'st thou?

Seru. No, my Lord. Nor sleepe nor wake.
But in a slumber troublesome to both.

D'am. Whence comes this gold?

Seru. 'Tis part of the Reuenew
Due to your Lordship since your brother's death.

D'am. To bed. Leaue me my gold.

Seru. And me my rest.
Two things wherewith one man is seldome blest.

Exit.

D'am. Cease that harsh musicke. W'are not pleas'd
with it.   [*He handles the gold.*
Heere sounds a musicke whose melodious touch
Like Angels' voices rauishes the sence.

Behold thou ignorant Astronomer
Whose wand'ring speculation seekes among
The planets for men's fortunes, with amazement
Behold thine errour and be planet strucke.
These are the Starres whose operations make
The fortunes and the destinies of men.
Yon lesser eyes of Heau'n (like Subjects rais'd
Into their loftie houses, when their Prince
Rides underneath th' ambition of their loues)
Are mounted onely to behold the face
Of your more rich imperious eminence
With unpreuented sight.   Unmaske, fair Queene.

                   [*Unpurses the gold.*

Vouchsafe their expectations may enjoy
The gracious fauour they admire to see.
These are the Starres the Ministers of Fate
And Man's high wisdome the superiour power
To which their forces are subordinate.   [*Sleepes.*

     Enter the Ghoast of MONTFERRERS.

Mont. D'amville !   With all thy wisedome th'art a foole.
     Not like those fooles that we terme innocents
     But a most wretched miserable foole

Which instantly, to the confusion of
Thy projects, with despaire thou shalt behold.

Exit Ghoast.

D'AMVILLE *starts up.*

D'am. What foolish dreame dares interrupt my rest
To my confusion ?   How can that be, since
My purposes haue hitherto beene borne
With prosp'rous Judgement to secure successe
Which nothing liues to dispossesse me of
But apprehended Charlemont.   And him
This braine has made the happy instrument
To free suspition, to annihilate
All interest and title of his owne
To seale up my assurance, and confirme
My absolute possession by the law.
Thus while the simple, honest worshipper
Of a phantastique prouidence, groanes under
The burthen of neglected miserie
My real wisedome has rais'd up a State
That shall eternize my posteritie.

Enter SERUANT *with the body of* SEBASTIAN.

What's that ?

Seru. The body of your younger Sonne
    Slaine by the Lord Belforest.

D'am. Slaine ! You lie !
    Sebastian ! Speak, *Sebastian !* He's lost
    His hearing. A Phisitian presently.
    Goe, call a Surgeon.

Rousa. Ooh.   [*Within.*

D'am. What groane was that ?
    How does my elder Sonne ? The sound came from
    His chamber.

Seru. He went sicke to bed, my Lord.

Rousa. Ooh.   [*Within.*

D'am. The cries of Mandrakes neuer touch'd the eare
    With more sad horrour than that voice does mine.

         Enter a Seruant running.

Seru. Neuer you will see your Sonne aliue——

D'am. Nature forbid I e'er should see him dead.

    [*A Bed drawne forth with* ROUSARD.]
    Withdraw the Curtaines. O how does my Sonne ?

Seru. Me thinkes he's ready to giue up the ghoast.

D'am. Destruction take thee and thy fatall tongue.

Dead ! where's the Doctor ? —— Art not thou
  the face
Of that prodigious apparition star'd upon
Me in my dreame ?

Seru. The Doctor's come, my Lord.   *Enter Doctor.*

D'am. Doctor, behold two Patients in whose cure
  Thy skill may purchase an eternal fame.
  If thou'st any reading in *Hipocrates,*
  Galen, or *Auicen;* if hearbs, or drugges,
  Or mineralles haue any power to saue,
  Now let thy practise and their soueraigne use
  Raise thee to wealth and honour.

Doct. If any roote of life remaines within 'em
  Capable of Phisicke feare 'em not, my Lord.

Rousa. Ooh.

D'am. His gasping sighes are like the falling noise
  Of some great building when the ground-worke
    breakes.
  On these two pillars stood the stately frame
  And architecture of my loftie house.
  An Earthquake shakes 'em. The foundation
    shrinkes.

Deare Nature, in whose honour I haue rais'd
A worke of glory to posteritie,
O burie not the pride of that great action
Under the fall and mine of it selfe.

Doct. My Lord, these bodies are depriu'd of all
The radicall abilitie of Nature.
The heat of life is utterly extinguish'd.
Nothing remaines within the power of man
That can restore them.

D'am. Take this gold, extract
The Spirit of it, and inspire new life
Into their bodies.

Doct. Nothing can, my Lord.

D'am. You ha' not yet examin'd the true state
And constitution of their bodies. Sure
You ha' not. I'll reserue their waters till
The morning. Questionlesse, their urines will
Informe you better.

Doct. Ha, ha, ha !

D'am. Dost laugh.
Thou villaine ? Must my wisdome that has beene
The obiect of men's admiration now
Become the subject of thy laughter ?

Rous. Ooh.   *Dies.*

  All. Hee's dead.

D'am. O there expires the date
        Of my posteritie !   Can Nature be
        So simple or malicious to destroy
        The reputation of her proper memorie?
        Shee cannot.   Sure there is some power aboue
        Her that controules her force.

Doct. A power aboue
        Nature ?   Doubt you that, my Lord ?   Consider
            but
        Whence Man receiues his body and his forme.
        Not from corruption like some wormes and flies,
        But onelie from the generation of
        A man.   For Nature neuer did bring forth
        A man without a man ; nor could the first
        Man, being but the passiue Subiect not
        The actiue Mouer, be the maker of
        Himselfe.   So of necessitie there must
        Be a superiour power to Nature.

D'am. Now to my selfe I am ridiculous.
        Nature thou art a Traytour to my soule.
        Thou hast abus'd my trust.   I will complaine

To a superior Court to right my wrong.
I'll proue thee a forger of false assurances.
In yon Starre chamber thou shalt answere it.
Withdraw the bodies.   O the sense of death
Begins to trouble my distracted soule.

Exeunt.

[SCENE II.]

Enter Judges and Officers.

1. *Judg.* Bring forth the malefactors to the Barre.

Enter CATAPLASMA, SOQUETTE, *and* FRESCO.

Are you the Gentlewoman in whose house
The murders were committed?

Catap. Yes, my Lord.

1. *Judg.* That worthie attribute of Gentrie which
Your habite drawes from ignorant respect
Your name deserues not, nor your selfe the name
Of woman, since you are the poyson that
Infects the honour of all womanhood.

Catap. My Lord, I am a Gentlewoman ; yet
I must confesse my pouertie compels
My life to a condition lower than
My birth or breeding.

2.*Judg.* Tush, we know your birth.

1.*Judg.* But, under colour to professe the Sale
       Of Tyres and toyes for Gentlewomen's pride,
       You draw a frequentation of men's wiues
       To your licentious house, and there abuse
       Their Husbands.——

Fresco. Good my Lord her rent is great.
       The good Gentlewoman has no other thing
       To liue by but her lodgings.   So she's forc'd
       To let her fore-roomes out to others, and
       Herselfe contented to lie backwards.

2.*Judg.* So.

1.*Judg.* Heere is no euidence accuses you
       For accessaries to the murder, yet
       Since from the Spring of lust, which you preseru'd
       And nourish'd, ranne th' effusion of that bloud,
       Your punishment shall come as neare to death
       As life can beare it   Law cannot inflict
       Too much seueritie upon the cause
       Of such abhor'd effects.

2.*Judg.* Receiue your sentence.
       Your goods (since they were gotten by that meanes
       Which brings diseases) shall be turn'd to th' use

Of Hospitalles. You carted through the Streetes
According to the common shame of strumpets
Your bodies whip'd, till with the losse of bloud
You faint under the hand of punishment.
Then that the necessarie force of want
May not prouoke you to your former life
You shall be set to painefull labour whose
Penurious gaines shall onely giue you foode
To hold up Nature, mortifie your flesh,
And make you fit for a repentant end.

All. O good my Lord !

1. *Judg.* No more.   Away with 'em.

  Exeunt CATAPLASMA, SOQUETTE, *and* FRESCO.

  Enter LANGUEBEAU SNUFFE.

2. *Judg.* Now, Monsieur Snuffe ! A man of your profession
  Found in a place of such impietie !

Snuffe. I grant you.   The place is full of impuritie.   So
  much the more neede of instruction and refor-
  mation.   The purpose that caried me thither
  was with the Spirit of conuersion to purifie their
  uncleanenesse, and I hope your Lordship will
  say the law cannot take hold o' me for that.

1. *Judg.* No, Sir, it cannot ; but yet giue me leaue
　　　To tell you that I hold your warie answere
　　　Rather premeditated for excuse
　　　Then spoken out of a religious purpose.
　　　Where tooke you your degrees of Schollership ?

Snuffe. I am no Scholler, my Lord.　To speake the sin-
　　　cere truth, I am Snuffe the Tallow-Chandler.

2. *Judg.* How comes your habits to be alter'd thus ?

Snuffe. My Lord Belforest, taking a delight in the cleane-
　　　nesse of my conuersation, withdrew mee from
　　　that uncleane life and put me in a garment fit
　　　for his societie and my present profession.

1. *Judg.* His Lordship did but paint a rotten post,
　　　Or couer foulenesse fairely.　Monsieur Snuffe,
　　　Back to your candle-making !　You may giue
　　　The world more light with that, then either with
　　　Instruction or th' example of your life.

Snuffe. Thus the Snuffe is put out.

　　　　　　　　　　　　　　　Exit SNUFFE.

Enter D'AMVILLE *distractedly with the hearses of his two*
　　　　　　Sonnes borne after him

D'am. Judgement ! Judgement !

2.*Judg.* Judgement, my Lord, in what?

D'am. Your Judgements must resolue me in a case.
Bring in the bodies. Nay, I'll ha' it tried.
This is the case, my Lord. By prouidence,
Eu'n in a moment, by the onely hurt
Of one, or two, or three at most, and those
Put quickly out o' paine too, marke mee, I
Had wisely rais'd a competent estate
To my posteritie. And is there not
More wisedome and more charity in that
Than for your Lordship, or your Father, or
Your Grandsire to prolong the torment and
The rack of rent from age to age upon
Your poore penurious Tenants, yet perhaps,
Without a pennie profit to your heire?
Is't not more wise? more charitable? Speake.

1.*Judg.* He is distracted.

D'am. How? distracted? Then
You ha' no Judgement. I can giue you sence
And solide reason for the very least
Distinguishable syllable I speake.
Since my thrift
Was more judicious than your Grandsires, why

I would faine know why your Lordship liues to
  make
A second generation from your Father,
And the whole frie of my posteritie
Extinguish'd in a moment.   Not a Brat
Left to succeede me.—I would faine know that.

2. *Judg.* Griefe for his children's death distempers him.

1. *Judg.* My Lord, we will resolue you of your question.
  In the meane time vouchsafe your place with us.

D'am. I am contented, so you will resolue me.—*Ascends.*

Enter CHARLEMONT *and* CASTABELLA.

2. *Judg.* Now, Monsieur Charlemont, you are accus'd
  Of hauing murder'd one Borachio, that
  Was seruant to my Lord D'amville.   How can
  You cleare your selfe?   Guiltie or not guiltie?

Charl. Guilty of killing him, but not of murder.
  My Lords, I haue no purpose to desire
  Remission for my selfe.——

                [D'amville *descends to* Charl.]

D'am. Unciuill Boy!
  Thou want'st humanitie to smile at griefe.

Why dost thou cast a chearefull eye upon
The object of my sorrow—my dead Sonnes?

1. *Judg.* O good my Lord, let Charitie forbeare
To vexe the spirit of a dying Man.
A chearefull eye upon the face of Death
Is the true count'nance of a noble minde.
For honour's sake, my Lord, molest it not.

D'am. Y'are all unciuill.   O ! is't not enough
That he uniustly hath conspir'd with Fate
To cut off my posteritie, for him
To be the heire to my possessions, but
He must pursue me with his presence.
And, in the ostentation of his ioy,
Laugh in my face and glory in my griefe ?

Charl. D'amville, to shew thee with what light respect
I value Death and thy insulting pride,
Thus, like a warlike Navie on the Sea
Bound for the conquest of some wealthie land,
Pass'd through the stormie troubles of this life,
And now arriu'd upon the armed coast
In expectation of the victorie
Whose honour lies beyond this exigent,

Through mortall danger, with an actiue spirit
Thus I aspire to undergoe my death.

> *Leapes up the Scaffold.*

> CASTABELLA *leapes after him.*

Casta. And thus I second thy braue enterprise.
Be chearefull, Charlemont.   Our liues cut off
In our young prime of yeares are like greene
      hearbes
Wherewith we strow the hearses of our friends.
For, as their vertue, gather'd when th'are greene,
Before they wither or corrupt, is best;
So we in vertue are the best for Death
While yet we haue not liu'd to such an age
That the encreasing canker of our sinnes
Hath spread too farre upon us.——

D'am. A Boone, my Lords.
I begge a Boone.

1. *Judg.* What's that, my Lord?

D'am. His body when 'tis dead
For an Anatomie.

2. *Judg.* For what, my Lord?

D'am. Your understanding still comes short o' mine.

I would finde out by his Anatomie
What thing there is in Nature more exact
Then in the constitution of my selfe.
Me thinkes my parts and my dimentions are
As many, as large, as well compos'd as his ;
And yet in me the resolution wants
To die with that assurance as he does.
The cause of that in his Anatomie
I would finde out.

1. *Judg.* Be patient and you shall.

D'am. I haue bethought me of a better way.
—Nephew, we must conferre.—Sir, I am growne
A wondrous Student now o' late.   My wit
Has reach'd beyond the scope of Nature, yet
For all my learning I am still to seeke
From whence the peace of conscience should
    proceede.

Charl. The peace of conscience rises in it selfe.

D'am. Whether it be thy Art or Nature I
Admire thee, Charlemont.   Why, thou hast taught
A woman to be valiant.   I will begge
Thy life.—My Lords, I begge my Nephewe's life.

Ile make thee my Phisitian.   Thou shalt read
Philosophie to me.   I will finde out
Th' efficient cause of a contented minde.
But if I cannot profit in't then 'tis
No more good being my Phisitian,
But infuse
A little poyson in a potion when
Thou giu'st me Phisick, unawares to me.
So I shall steale into my graue without
The understanding or the feare of death.
And that's the end I aime at.   For the thought
Of death is a most fearefull torment ; is it not ?

2. *Judg.* Your Lordship interrupts the course of law.

1. *Judg.* Prepare to die.

Charl. My resolution's made.
But ere I die, before this honour'd bench,
With the free voice of a departing soule,
I heere protest this Gentlewoman cleare
Of all offence the law condemnes her for.

Casta. I haue accus'd my selfe.   The law wants power
To cleare me.   My deare Charlemont, with thee
I will partake of all thy punishments.

Charl. Uncle, for all the wealthie benefits
   My death aduances you, graunt me but this :
   Your mediation for the guiltlesse life
   Of Castabella, whom your conscience knowes
   As justly cleare, as harmlesse innocence.

D'am. Freely. My Mediation for her life
   And all my int'rest in the world to boote ;
   Let her but in exchange possesse me of
   The resolution that she dies withall.
   —The price of things is best knowne in their
    want.
   Had I her courage, so I value it :
   The Indies should not buy 't it out o' my hands.

Charl. Giue mee a glasse of water.

D'am. Mee of wine.——
   This argument of death congeales my bloud.
   Colde feare, with apprehension of thy end,
   Hath frozen up the riuers of my veines.—

       A glasse of wine given him.

   I must drinke wine to warme me and dissolue ,
   The obstruction ; or an apoplexie will
   Possesse mee.—Why, thou uncharitable Knaue,

Dost thou bring mee bloud to drinke ?   The very glasse
Lookes pale and trembles at it.

Seru. 'Tis your hand, my Lord.

D'am. Canst blame mee to be fearefull, bearing still
The presence of a murderer about me ?

Charl. Is this water ?

Seru. Water, Sir.   —*A glasse of water.*

Charl. Come, thou cleare embleme of coole temperance,
Be thou my witnesse that I use no art
To force my courage nor haue neede of helpes
To raise my Spirits, like those weaker men
Who mixe their bloud with wine, and out of that
Adulterate coniunction doe beget
A bastard valour.   Natiue courage, thankes.
Thou lead'st me soberly to undertake
This great hard worke of magnanimitie.

D'am. Braue Charlemont, at the reflexion of
Thy courage my cold fearefull bloud takes fire
And I begin to emulate thy death.
—Is that thy executioner ?   My Lords,

You wrong the honour of so high a bloud
To let him suffer by so base a hand.

Judges. He suffers by the forme of law, my Lord.

D'am. I will reforme it. Downe, you shagge-hair'd curre.
The instrument that strikes my nephew's bloud
Shall be as noble as his blood. I'll be
Thy executioner my selfe.

1. *Judg.* Restraine his fury. Good my Lord, forbeare.

D'am. I'll butcher out the passage of his soule
That dares attempt to interrupt the blow.

2. *Judg.* My Lord, the office will impresse a marke
Of scandall and dishonour on your name.

Charl. The office fits him : hinder not his hand,
But let him crowne my resolution with
An unexampled dignitie of death.
Strike home. Thus I submit me.

[Readie for Execution.]

Casta. So doe I.
In scorne of Death thus hand in hand we die.

D'am. I ha' the trick on 't, Nephew. You shall see
How eas'ly I can put you out of paine.—Ooh !

As he raises up the Axe strikes out his owne braines.
Staggers off the Scaffold.

Execu. In lifting up the Axe
  I thinke h's knock'd his brains out.

D'am. What murderer was hee that lifted up
  My hand against my head?

Judge. None but your selfe, my Lord.

D'am. I thought he was a murderer that did it.

Judge. God forbid!

D'am. Forbid? You lie, Judge. He commanded it.
  To tell thee that man's wisedome is a foole.
  I came to thee for Judgement, and thou think'st
  Thy selfe a wise man. I outreach'd thy wit
  And made thy Justice Murder's instrument
  In Castabella's death and Charlemont's.
  To crowne my Murder of Montferrers with
  A safe possession of his wealthie state

Charl. I claime the just aduantage of his words.

Judge. Descend the Scaffold, and attend the rest.

D'am. There was the strength of naturall understanding.
  But Nature is a foole. There is a power

Above her that hath ouerthrowne the pride
Of all my proiects and posteritie,
For whose suruiuing bloud
I had erected a proud monument,
And struck 'em dead before me. For whose deathes
I call'd to thee for Judgement.   Thou didst want
Descretion for the sentence.   But yon power
That strucke me knew the Judgement I deseru'd,
And gave it.—O ! the lust of Death commits
A Rape upon me as I would ha' done
On Castabella.

Dies.

Judge.   Strange is his death and iudgement. With the hands
Of Joy and Justice I thus set you free.
The power of that eternall prouidence
Which ouerthrew his proiects in their pride
Hath made your griefes the instruments to raise
Your blessings to a greater height then euer.

Charl.   Only to Heau'n I attribute the worke,
Whose gracious motiues made me still forbeare
To be mine owne Reuenger.   Now I see
That *Patience is the honest man's reuenge.*

Judge In stead of Charlemont that but e'en now
    Stood readie to be dispossess'd of all
    I now salute you with more titles both
    Of wealth and dignitie, then you were borne to.
    And you, sweet Madame, Lady of *Belforest*,
    You haue that title by your Father's death.

Casta. With all the titles due to me encrease
    The wealth and honour of my Charlemont
    Lord of Montferrers, Lord D'amville Belforest,—
    And for a cloze to make up all the rest—*Embrace.*
    The Lord of Castabella.   Now at last
    Enioy the full possession of my loue,
    As cleare and pure as my first chastitie.

Charl. The crowne of all my blessings !—I will tempt
    My Starres no longer, nor protract my time
    Of marriage.   When those Nuptiall rites are
    done
    I will performe my kinsmen's funeralles.

Judg. The Drums and Trumpets ! Interchange the
    sounds
    Of Death and Triumph. For these honour'd
    lives,

Succeeding their deserued Tragedies.

Charl. Thus, by the worke of Heau'n, the men that
    thought
    To follow our dead bodies without teares
    Are dead themselves, and now we follow theirs.

                                Exeunt.

FINIS.

NOTES TO THE ATHEIST'S TRAGEDIE.

ACT I.

Borachio. Borachio properly means a drunkard. Cf. Middleton's *Spanish Gipsy*—"I am no Borachio, sach, malaga, nor Canary breeds the calenture in my brains."

But where that favour, etc.

Appearance, countenance, or quality, exactly the Latin *species;* for the first meaning cf. Marlowe's *Hero and Leander*, sect. 4 : "From the sweet conduits of her *favour* fell," and infra, act i. sc. iii., "Methinks you have a sweet *favour* of your own." For the second meaning cf. *Lear*, act i. sc. iv., "This admiration, sir, is much of the *favour* of your other pranks."

And with a sweet, etc.

Ovid has expressed the same sentiment with the coarser realism of a Roman, *Amores*, ii. 10.

Your commandëment.

For the lengthening of the syllable see note on *Revenger's Tragedy*, act i. sc. i.

Invites to breakfast.

This was a somewhat exceptional meal, as we learn from Holinshead's *Chronicles*, vol. i. p. 287, "Whereas of old we had breakfasts in the fore-noon, beverages or nuntions after dinner. Now these old repasts, thanked be God, are verie well left out, and each one in manner contenteth himself with dinner and supper only."

Where I to choose, etc.

This is evidently an aposiopesis, and as such I have punctuated.

To bring you on the way.

Escort you ; cf. note on *Revenger's Trag.* act i., " you'll bring me on the way."

She's like your diamond, etc.

Tourneur and Mr. Browning must divide the palm of exquisite application, and have given as lovely significance to this gem as Landor and Wordsworth have to the sea shell. See Mr. Browning's little poem entitled *Magical Nature*, in his last volume.

By that I am confirmed an Atheist.

This foolish remark is one of the many instances of the puerility so common in this play.

And instantly, etc.

This is printed as prose, and so also is the whole of Languebeau's speech, which follows. I have restored the blank verse.

Begotten by conceit.

In the common sense of imagination.

The hinges oiled.

Cf. *Malecontent,* act i. sc. ii., " oiled hinges and all the tongue-tied lascivious witnesses of great creatures' wantonness."

The Athenian ladies resorted to the simpler expedient of watering the hinges :

" ἐγὼ δε καταχέασα τõν στροφέως ὕδωρ
ἐξῆλθον ὡς τὸν μοιχόν,"

as Aristophanes informs us in a passage which is an excellent, though indirect commentary on Tourneur's text, see the *Thesmophoriazusæ,* 477—489.

ACT II.

A considerable time must obviously be supposed to have elapsed between the first and second act.

The Enemies defeated, etc.

What follows is a description of the siege of Ostend, taken literally from what happened at that memorable scene. Allusions to this siege are very common in the Dramatists: among many others there are three in the *Return from Parnassus.* Webster's *Westward Ho,* act i. sc. i., "How long will you hold out, think you? Not so long as Ostend," and act iv. sc. ii. See too the Notes on Tourneur's *Funeral Poem on Sir Francis Vere; passim,* and çf. *A True Historie of the Memorable Siege of Ostend,* London, 1604. The following passages from Sir Francis Vere's *Commentaries* with the Supplement, containing Henry Hexam's Account, may be compared with the text, "General Vere perceiving the enemy to fall off commanded me to run as fast as ever I could to Serjeant-Major Carpenter and the auditour Fleming, who were upon Helmont, that they should presently open the west sluice, out of which there ran such a stream and torrent down thorugh the channel of the West Haven, that upon their retreat it carried away many of their sound and hurt men into the sea.

*   *   *   *   *   *   *

"Under Sandhill and all along the walls of the old town, the Porcepsic and west raveline, lay whole heaps of dead carcases, forty or fifty upon a heap, stark naked. There lay also upon the sand dead horses," &c.

There are also other little points and particulars which Tourneur has seized. It is not impossible that Tourneur, when engaged in his poem on Vere, may have seen this work in MS., for though it was not published till 1657, Dr. Dillingham, its first editor, informs us that there were many MS. copies in circulation.

Walking one day upon the fatal shore.

See Lamb's note on this passage.

"This way of description, which seems unwilling ever to leave off weaving parenthesis within parenthesis, was brought to its height by Sir Philip Sidney. He seems to have set the example to Shakespeare. Many beautiful instances may be found all over the *Arcadia.* These bountiful wits always give full measure, pressed down and overflowing."

See Alexander Smith's *Life Drama,* sc. ii., where he is said to have plagiarised from the passage in the text.

With Tourneur's description may also be compared a singularly beautiful passage in Minucius Felix, *Octavius,* cap. ii.

Thou art a scrichowle.

Cf. Webster's *Dutchess of Malfi,* act iii. sc. ii.—

"The howling of a wolf
Is music to thee scrichowle."

This bird's claim to being ill-omened are fully entered into by Ovid in his *Fasti,* vi. 139 seqq.

My Lord the Jacks abused me.

See Halliwell's exhaustive article on this word, *Dictionary,* vol. i. p. 1.; and compare Middleton's *Women beware of Women,* act i. sc. i.—

"I did it, then he set Jackes on me."

Clap him on the coxcombe.

This was properly a fool's-cap with its cock's-feathers, then it came to mean simply the head. Cf. Ford's Sun's Darling, act ii. sc. iii.—

"'Twas his humour
The knight broke his coxcombe."

Eternal darkness damn you.

All this and the speech of D'Amville, as well as the following speeches are printed as prose in the quarto, the blank verse is restored.

Here's a sweet comedy.

In the next two speeches the blank verse is restored.

Begins with O dolentis.

With the O of one in pain ; cf. heus admirantis, etc., an odd and tragical application of a rule from Latin Grammar.

Till I had perished my sound lungs.

It is here an active verb, as often ; cf. Ford *Fancies Chaste and Noble*—

　　"But if you have not *perish'd* all your reason ;"

and—

　　"And miseries have *perished* his good face,"

　　　　FLETCHER'S *Honest Man's Fortune,* act i. sc. i.

An exhalation hot and drie, etc.

This is taken from Lucretius ; cf. *De Rer. Nat.*, vi. 270 seqq. I restore the blank verse limping though it be.

Our next endeavour, etc.

In this and the following speech I restore the blank verse.

Manned. Attended.

Prithee untie my shoe.

The same point is made by Sterne in his *Sentimental Journey,* though the fille de chambre and Levidulcia would seem to have little in common. The whole of this scene may be compared with one of a similar kind in *Joseph Andrewes.*

Candied suckets, a sort of conserve or sweet-meat.

Cf. *Marstone,* Sec. Part of *Anton. and Mellita,* act v. sc. v.—

　　"Bring hither *suckets,* candied delicates."

My husband he grew so in a rage, etc.

This device of Levidulcia's for conveying Sebastian and Fresco out of her chamber when surprised by Belleforest is taken from Boccaccio's *Decameron, 7,* novel 6.

And I having shifted, etc.

It would appear from Marston first pt. of *Anton. and Mellita,* act ii. sc. i., that it was considered eccentric and dirty to wear socks.

And bid him hang himself in his own garters.

As Falstaff bade the Prince do, first pt. of Henry IV. act ii. sc. ii., " Go hang thyself in thine own heir-apparent garters."

Why, 'tis a music, etc.

Here again, as well as in the following speech, the blank verse is restored.

Our boyling phantasies.

This attempt of Charlemont to give a scientific explanation of an imaginary delusion may be compared with Clermont's ; see Chapman's *Revenge of Bussy D'Ambois*, act v. sc. i. The whole theory of dreams is learnedly discussed by Lodge—*Fig for Momus*—Epistle to W. Bolton.

Stand, stand I say. Here again the blank verse is restored.

ACT III.

A practique.

The old way of spelling practice. See Gifford's note on Massinger *Emperor of the East*, act ii. sc. i.—

" He has the theory only, not the *practique;*"

and Heywood, *English Traveller*, act i. sc. i.—

" I have the theorique, but you the *practique*."

The altar of his tomb, etc.

This is a direct plagiarism from *Two Gentlemen of Verona*, act iii. sc. ii.—

" Say that upon the altar of her beauty
You sacrifice your tears."

Cf. also Marlowe's *Jew of Malta*, act iii.—

" Let them be interred
Within one sacred monument of stone ;
Upon which altar I will offer up
My daily sacrifice of sighs and tears."

See also Æschylus, *Choephoræ*, 104, to whom the original image belongs.

I feel a substance warm, etc.

This scene may be compared with the corresponding scene in the *Electra* of Sophocles, where Orestes and Electra meet. *Electra,* 1176, *seqq.*

Marry'd ?—Had not my mother, etc.

This is one of the many passages where Tourneur's purely sensual conception of the passion of love is disagreeably forced upon us. But it is curious to see how here and elsewhere where the mean is transgressed the extremes will often meet. Asceticism and sensuality will express themselves sometimes in the same disagreeable paradoxes. "The philosopher may be excused," writes an amiable and reverend translator of Plato, in his Introduction to the *Republic,* "if he imagines an age when poetry and sentiment have disappeared, and truth has taken the place of imagination, and the feelings of love" (which he defines as "the illusion of the senses commonly called love") "are understood and estimated at their proper value."

Y'are excellent at crying of a rape.

Cf. act i. sc. iii., *ad finem.*

What wounded. Blank verse restored.

Use of serjeants.

A serjeant is a sheriff's officer. Cf. *Tr. Meta.*—

"Ere serjeant death will call me at my dore."

Trebles and bases make poor music without means, etc.

These are of course plays upon the musical terms : the mean answered to the tenor. For precisely the same play upon the words, cf. Lyly's *Gallathea,* act v. sc. iii.—

"*Venus.* Can you sing?

Raffe. Basely.

Venus. And you?

Dicke. Meanly.

Venus. And what can you doe?

Rolin. If they double it, I will *treble* it ;"

and cf. also *Witch of Edmonton,* act i. sc. i., and *Two Gentlemen of Verona,* act iv. sc. iv.

O Father Mercy.

This speech is of course modelled closely on Portia's *Merchant of Venice,* act iv. sc. i. But cf. Sophocles *Œd. Col.,* 1270—

> " Ἀλλ' ἔστι γὰρ καὶ Ζηνὶ σύνθακος θρόνων
> 'Αιδὼς ἔπ' ἔργοις πᾶσι καὶ πρὸς σὸι, πάτερ
> Παρασταθήτω."

ACT IV.

How conceited you are.

Witty, or facetious. Cf. Massinger, *Bondman,* act ii. sc. i.—

" You are grown *conceited.*"

The reader will excuse a commentary on this passage.

Mi is a *laerg* there. The reprint reads large. Perhaps he means *Iago.*

The prick that, etc.

See Reed's note on the *Sun's Darling,* act ii. sc. i., and seriously consult Sir John Hawkins' *Hist. of Music,* vol. ii. p. 243.

Falls and tyres.

The same play is made on these words in the *Malcontent,* act v. sc. iii.—" Look you these *tiring* things are justly out of request now : you must wear *falling*-bands ; you must into the *falling* fashion.

See *Lingua* and Lyly's *Mydas,* act i. sc. i., for an almost exhaustive catalogue of the attire and ornaments of the ladies of this time. The *shadow* is the same thing as a Bonegrace or the border attached to a bonnet or projecting hat to defend the complexion. Cotgrave defines the word to be "a fashion of shadow or bornegrace used in old time and at this day by some old women." See Halliwell. Cf. Jordan's *Death Dissected*—

> " For your head here's precious gear,
> Bone lace, crosclothes, squares and shadows."

A tire is a head-dress, see note on the *Revenger's Tragedy*.   The fall was a sort of veil ; the same as the French *faille,* which is defined by Cotgrave as " the round and out-bearing *faile* worn by nuns and widows of the better sort.

This pistoll.   There is the same play on the word discharge in *Henry IV.,* part ii. act ii. sc. iv.

Like a superfluous letter in the law.

Cf. *Lear,* act ii. sc. ii.—" Thou Zed, thou unnecessary letter.

Perhaps he's praying, then he's fit to die, etc.

A reminiscence, doubtless, of the celebrated passage in *Hamlet,* act iii. sc. iii.

Tis—have I.   The quarto reads " this" and reverses the words have I.

How fit a place, etc.

In this speech of Charlemont's—modelled, of course, on Hamlet's— prose and blank verse are so confused that it is difficult to disentangle them.   Where the distinction is obvious I print it as blank verse.   There is a very fine parody on the Hamlet scene on which this is modelled in Randolph's *Jealous Lovers,* act iv. sc. ii. and iii., which in its bitter and angry cynicism is more like the Tourneur of the *Revenger's Tragedy* than anything I know.

What, have I killed him, etc.   Blank verse restored.

This disguise.   Tourneur was probably indebted for this particular kind of humour to *Merrie Boccace.*

What ha' we heere, etc.   Blank verse restored.

My Lord, the night, etc.

In the following speeches the blank verse is restored.

A man, and such a man, etc.

Here again verse and prose is entangled, but in the two following speeches I restore the blank verse, so also in Castabella's long

speech and D'Amville's answer, and again in Castabella's second
speech, "Suppos'd protection," etc. To the end of the scene I have
restored the blank verse.

Nature allows, etc.

D'Amville is indebted for his damnable sophistry to Ovid, *Met.* x.
324 *seqq.* Goethe and Ford have more elaborate arguments for a
parallel and kindred horror.

Did but paint a rotten post.

Cf. Marston, *Scourge of Villainy,* sat. x.—
" *Paint not a rotten post* with colours rich."

Bill. The bill was a broad-bladed implement on the end of a
staff carried by watchmen. Cf. Lyly's *Endimion,* act iv. sc. ii., and
see Halliwell's note. There is of course a play on the words.

O God, my husband.

Here again the blank verse is restored, as also in parts of the pre-
ceding speeches.

Levidulcia's dying speech is evidently modelled on the last speeches
of Isabella in Marston's *Insatiate Countess,* act v.

The sea wants water, etc.

This image, appropriated by Shakespeare, belongs to Æschylus.
Cf. *Choephoræ,* 70—

" Πόροι τε πάντες ἐκ μιᾶς ὁδοῦ
Βάινοντες τὸν χαιρομυσῆ
Φόνον καθάιροντες ἰοῦσαν ἄτην."

ACT V.

The gracious favour. See note on act i. sc. i.

They *admire* to see. Wonder, as often. Cf. Milton, *Paradise
Lost,* bk. i. 690—

" Let none *admire* that riches grow in hell."

Apprehended Charlemont. A not uncommon Latinism.

The cries of mandrakes.

"The mandrake has been supposed to be a creature having life and engendered under the earth, of the seed of some dead person that hath been convicted or put to death for some felony or murder, and that they had the same in such dampish and funeral places where the said convicted persons were buried."—Thomas Newton, *Herbal to the Bible*, 1587. It was said also to cry out if it were pulled up, and there was a superstition that any one who heard the cry went mad. Cf. *Duchess of Malfi*, act ii. sc. v., "I have this night digged up a mandrake, and I'm grown mad with 't." Allusions to it are very common : see *Romeo and Juliet*, act iv. sc. iii. ; sec. part *Henry VI.*, act iii. sc. ii. ; sec. part *Henry IV.*, act i. sc. ii. It is sometimes alluded to merely as a drug, see Massinger, *Unnatural Combat*, act i. sc. i.—

> "Though she had drunk opium
> Or eaten mandrakes."

Cf. also Sir Thomas Browne, *Vulgar Errors*, bk. ii. chap. 6. Allusions to it in this connection are very common. It is Shakespeare's *mandragora*. All through this scene I have restored the blank verse.

The body of your younger son, etc.

From here to the end of the scene I restored the blank verse, often a matter of no small difficulty.

In yon starre-chamber. A play of course on the word.

A frequentation, Lat. frequentatio, an assembly or crowding. In this and Fresco's speech blank verse restored.

Your judgments must restore me. In this and D'Amville's second speech I restore blank verse. *My* providence I alter into *by*.

We will resolve you, etc.

Satisfy or inform ; cf. Ford, *Honest Whore*, act ii. sc. ii., "*Resolve* thyself it will ;" and third part *Henry VI.*, act iii. sc. ii., "May it please your highness to *resolve* me now."

Uncivil boy.

This is a very beautiful touch. The blank verse is restored both in this and in D'Amville's next speech.

This exigent. Exigency, or extremity.

See *A Merry Trick to know a Knave,* " And, God willing, their good names shall never take an *exigent* in me ;" also *Lady Alimony,* act iii. scene i., " Yet reduced to this strait and sad *exigent.*"

That the increasing canker.

In these beautiful lines is the germ of Coleridge's *Epitaph on a Child ;* though he had probably never seen this work.

Still comes. So the reprint rightly for come.

I have bethought me. Blank verse restored.

Whether it be, etc.

Here again I restore blank verse. After " no more" I insert the word " good," which has probably dropped out of the text.

This argument of death, etc. Cf., among many more, *Timon,* act ii. sc. ii., " And try the *arguments* of hearts by borrowing."

Brave Charlemont, etc. In the next two speeches the blank verse is restored ; so also in D'Amville's speech, " Forbid ? you lie," etc.

A

FUNERALL POEME

Upon the

Death of the Most Worthie

And True Sovldier,

Sir FRANCIS VERE, Knight;

Captaine of Portsmouth, &c., L. Gouernour of
his Maiesties Cautionarie Towne of
Briell in Holland, &c.

L O N D O N:
Printed for *Eleazar Edgar.*
1609.

A FUNERALL POEM.

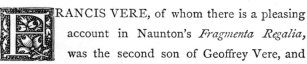RANCIS VERE, of whom there is a pleasing
account in Naunton's *Fragmenta Regalia,*
was the second son of Geoffrey Vere, and
the grandson of John Vere, Earl of Oxford. He
was born in 1558, and after the ordinary education
entered the army. In his twenty-seventh year he
enrolled himself among the forces sent by Queen Elizabeth to assist the States of Holland, under the command of the Earl of Leicester, Dec. 10th, 1585. In
this expedition he distinguished himself for his courage
and that extraordinary presence of mind which characterised the whole of his military career, and is so particularly enlarged on by Tourneur. But it was at the
siege of Sluys, in 1587, that his brilliant services brought
him prominently into notice. With a handful of English
and Walloons, he and Sir Roger Williams (see notes)

kept at bay the collective forces of the Prince of Parma, and defended the town against the incessant attacks of an enemy who had already thrown into it seventeen thousand great-shot and made a large breach in the walls.

In the following year he made a conspicuous figure at the siege of Bergen-op-Zoom, and, to borrow Camden's words—" That true courage might not want its due reward or distinction, the Lord Willoughby, who was general of the English after Leicester's departure, conferred the honour of knighthood on Sir Francis Vere, whose great fame commenced from that siege." He performed splendid services in the affair of Bergh (1589), at the Castle of Lickenhooven, in the Fort of Recklinchusen (1590); and the following year he took by stratagem a fort near Zutphen, which did much to facilitate the siege of that important place. In 1596 he was recalled from the Low Countries and appointed Lord-Marshal of the army sent against Cadiz. Of this campaign he has in his *Commentaries* given a minute account. As they were setting out he came into collision with Sir Walter Raleigh on a point of etiquette, which reversing the usual process in such matters, began with a quarrel and ended with a joke.

The success of the English against the Spaniards in this expedition is said to have been indebted in no small degree to the bravery and military skill of Vere, though disinterested historians have not always been so ready to acknowledge his claims as interested biographers.

On his return to England, Elizabeth made him Governor of Briel (December, 1597), much to the annoyance of some of her noble courtiers, who considered the election of a commoner to so high an office a slight to themselves. Their indignation was no doubt aggravated when the Governorship of Portsmouth was added to his other honours.

The two memorable exploits which signalise the latter years of his war-worn life were the battle of Newport, in 1600, and the siege of Ostend in 1601 (see notes). He died in London, August 28th, 1608, and is interred in St. John's Chapel, Westminster Abbey. Vere, like his first patron, Sir Roger Williams, has left an account of his military exploits in his *Commentaries,* which embody much interesting matter in an unusually dull style.

A FUNERALL POEME

VPON THE DEATH OF

THE MOST WORTHEY AND

TRUE SOVLDIER SIR FRANCIS

VERE, KNIGHT: CAPTAINE OF PORTSMOUTH, ETC.

LORD GOUERNOUR OF HIS MAIESTIES CAUTIONARIE

TOWNE OF BRIELL IN HOL

LAND ETC.

THY earth's return'd to earth, from whence it came,
But from thy spirit rizze* thy worthy fame,
Immortal Vere; and that shall never dye
But with it live to all Posteritie.

How can the memory of such a spirit,—
Whose actions ev'n of envy got his merit
Acknowledgement, subscription, approbation,
And made it clearly shine through emulation,
Which with contracted cloudes did interpose
Betweene the world and him, to darken those

---

* Rizze—the old form of the preterite. See amid many other
instances, Ben Johnson :
      "For I am *risse* here with a covetous hope
      To blast your pleasures."—*Poetaster :* Introduction.

Illustrious honours of his noble worth
Which his essential souldiership brought forth—
Be ever ruin'd ?   Nor can Death or Fate
Confine his fame to an expiring date,
Since all they can doe is to kill his earth
Whose dust, wip'd of his soule, a second birth
Regenerates the honour of his acts
Unto eternity.   He that detracts
The dead man's good, defames his owne intent
And makes obscurèd virtues eminent.
But, noble Vere, this monument I raise
With uncorrupted purpose to thy praise.
All that I speak is unexacted, true and free
Drawne clearely from unalter'd certaintee,
For heere I do ingenuously professe
The nature of this subject would oppresse
And trouble my reposèd state of soule,
With contemplating that which should control*
Our licenses of conscience, if the due
Of this I áttribute† thee, were untrue.

* Original contruleo.
† Accent on the first syllable, as often in the old writers, cf.
Spenser, F. Q., vol. iv. 28 :
    " But faulty men use oftentimes
        To attribute their folly unto fate."

And you the worthies of our present daies,
Whose judgements and experience knew his ways
Conversèd with his actions, and intents
In private and in publique managements :
To your true understandings it is knowne
That he might claim these honours from his owne.
His Minde was like an Empire, rich and strong
In all defensive power against the wrong
That civil tumult or invasive Hate
Might raise against the peace of her estate.
It was a plentifull and fertile ground
Wherein all needfull riches did abound.
Labour increas'd what natively was bred
No part was barren, or ill-husbandèd.
And with the paines of industry and witt
In little time he made such benefit
Of conversation, (the commerce of minds)
That what his hable* observation finds
In other knowledges of use and good
Which in his owne was yet not understood.
Through this rich trade—whereby all good is known—

* Hable, fit, proper.   Cf. old French habil, and Latin habilis.

Converts them home and plantes them in his own
Which was so sweet and temperate a seate,
Without th' extremities of cold or heate
That it could easily itselfe apply
To ev'ry usefull Nature properlie,
And so did yield such prosperous increase
Of virtues qualifi'd for warre and peace
That not a mind wherewith he did conferre
Could utter speech of that particular,
Though in the waies which other men profess'd,
Wherewith his understanding was not bless'd ;
And whatsoever he deliver'd forth
In serious things was of a solide worth
Commodiously materiall ; full of use ;
And free from ostentation and abuse

And as that Empire of his minde was good
So was her state as strong wherein she stood.
Her situation most entirely lay
Within itselfe, admitting not a way
Nor any open place, infirme or weake
By which offensive purposes might breake

Into her government, or have accesse*
Thorough the most familiar passages
That led upon him, under faire pretence
Without discovering they meant offence.
Before it was too late to give retreat
To their proceedings.   Nor could any heate
Or violence of such invasion make
His passions mutin' or his powers forsake
Their proper places.   Nothing could disband
The strength and order of his mind's command.
For never mind her nature better knew
Or could observe a discipline more due
To such a nature, or was fortified
With workes were more ingeniously applied
To answere all attempts and injuries
In their owne kinde and sev'ral qualities.

* Tourneur seems particularly fond of this rhyme, cf. below:
       "Nor need I from this martial scope digress
           T' approve that by his morall cariges ;"
and again :
       "Whereas his nature did itselfe expresse
           Adapted unto publique bus'neses ;"
and :
       "Out of their proper seats and offices
           Into a narrow lymitt where the presse," &c.

And in that scope, offences to avoid,
The use of all those forces was employ'de.
Within his Nature's lines it might be read
He was a souldier borne as well as bred,
And out of his owne morall character
He might have learn'd his mysterie of warre.

Warre was the spheare wherein his life did moove,
And in that course his actions did approove,
How well his worth did his employment fit
Th'* united provinces can witness it,
And will acknowledge gratefully that fate
Was graciously propicious to their state,
When their most happie genius gave their voice
And did direct their wisedomes to make choice
Of one so hable and so fit in all
To be that worthy nation's generall,
On the sufficiencie of whose command
The chiefest hopes of their successe did stand

And noble Willoughby† thy judgement knew
And he hath rëallie confirm'd it true

* See the Introduction.
† Peregrine Lord Willoughby was the son of Richard Berlie and
his wife Catherine, daughter and sole heir of William Willoughby,

That in his life thy memorie should live
For the judicious favours thou didst give
To his beginnings, which did still produce
Some action promising of what high use
His generous courage, wit and industrie
Practiz'd with judgment and dexteritie
Should be unto that state.   In whose brave warre,
When he had brought his services so farre
That they deserv'd the chiefest English charge,
His spirit with his fortune did enlarge
Itselfe according to his place.   For as

Lord Willoughby of Eresby, and was born October 12th, 1555.
On the death of his mother he laid claim to the title he inherited
from her and it was granted. His first great military engagement
was the siege of Zutphen, in 1587, where he defeated and took
prisoner George Cressiak, Commander in Chief of the enemy's
horse. In 1588, having been appointed general of the auxiliary
forces in the United Provinces, he distinguished himself by his
vigorous defence of Bergen-op-Zoom, which was then being besieged
by the Prince of Parma. It was here that Vere's courage and
ability first brought him into notice. " And that true courage might
not want its due reward or distinction, the Lord Willoughby conferred the honour of knighthood on Sir Francis Vere, whose fame
commenced from this siege "—the judicious favour alluded to in
the text. As he had married Mary, daughter of John Vere Earl of
Oxford, he was related to Sir Francis. He died in 1601. The manly
independence of his character is pleasantly illustrated by an anecdote
in Naunton's *Fragmenta Regalia.*

His former carriages did duely passe
Through those right waies by which he should obey
Now he did proove he knew as right a way
How to command, and suited all his course
With correspondent order, life and force.

He put not on these popular aspects
Which great-ness oft obsequiously affectes
To win the vulgar fancie ; for he knew
That humour would distract him from the true
And faithful course wherein he should attend
The publique service to a private ende,
And with too easie and familiar sense
Make favour apprehended, and dispence
With such neglect of dutie as proceedes
From that presumption which remissness breedes,
But gave himself unto the publique cause,
And in the due performance of her Lawes
His favours had their constant residence
To th' end he might attract mens' diligence
Directly to their duties, and advance
The armies service.   For his countenance
Respected men with a reservednesse
Refer'd to that wherewith he did expresse

His exemplarie actions, so that none
Could gather from him any signe whereon
To raise themselves a promise or a hope
Of their preferment, but within the scope
Of their peculiar merites.   And the waies
And manner by the which he us'd to raise
Deserving men, and did his favour spread
Were with as much discretion managèd,
And nourish'd industry no less.   For whan
He did bestow preferment on a man
The gift descended from no second hand
That might divide a general command ;
But from himselfe, as a proprietie
Reserv'd unto his own authoritie
And often, unrequested, singled forth
Some private men, whom for desert and worth
He did advance to some employment fit,
Before they sought it or expected it.
Hence did his troupes not only understand
Their hopes* to rise depended on his hand

* Cf. *Atheist Tragedy*, act i. sc. ii. :
        " *Her power to speak* is perish'd in her tears ;"
and :
        " *His fame to be severe* contemned at," etc., *infra*.

But that he carried an observing eie
That would informe him how deservingly
They bore themselves, which did as well produce
Endeavour to do well, as curbe abuse,
And made example emulation breed
Which, leading unto generous ends doth feede
The active disposition of 'he spirit
With a desire to goe beyond in merit.
In which pursuit his action still was wont
To lead the way to honour.   And i' the front
Of danger where he did his deeds advance
In all his gestures and his countenance
He did so pleasing a consent expresse
Of noble courage and free cheerfulnesse
That his assurance had the power to raise
The most dejected spirit into praise
And imitation of his worth.   And thus
By means heroique and judicious
He did incline his armie's gen'rous part
With love unto the practise of desert.
And in that mooving orbe of active warre
His high command was the transcendent starre
Whose influence, for production of mens worthes,

Did governe at their militarie birthes
And made them fit for arms.   Witness the merits
Ev'n of the chiefest ranckes of war-like spirits
Who for our Prince's service do survive
Which from his virtues did their worthes derive.

Then, to reduce th' affections of the rude
And ill-dispos'd licentious multitude
His wisedome likewise did as amplie show
Tradition and experience made him know
That men in armies are more apt t' offend
And faults to greater danger doe extend
There than in civill governments and are
More difficult to be suppress'd in warre
Than peace ; and that there's nothing can restrain
Their dissolute affections but the reine
Of strict and exemplarie punishment.
Since of necessitie such governement
Must bee: his entrance therefor was severe
Which did possess them with a timelie feare.
For when a chiefe comes first into his place
Then all men's eies are bent upon the face
Of his behaviour with a fix'd regard,
In which attention they are best prepar'd

To take impression what they ought to doe
That he would have them be accustom'd to.
For as his manners then report him, so
The reputation of his name will go.
And thus his name grew hable to suppresse
The strong'st commotions of licenciousness,
E'en in their first conceptions.   Or if some
Were still so bold to undergoe his doome,
Yet in the terroor of his very name
They were so long projecting how to frame
And execute their practise safe and free
Without the danger of severitee,
That if their doubtfulness did not divert
And utterly disanimate the heart
Of their proceedings ; yet their coldness brought
The act so impotentlie from the thought
And made their strong'st performances so lame
That they were overtaken, e're they came
To prejudice the publique cause.   And now,
When as the few complaints reported how
Effectually his labours prosper'd, and
His men grew well conform'd to his command ;
With their obedience he did slacke the bent

Of his severitie in punishment,
Yet with so wise a moderation that
His fame to be severe continu'd at
The full opinion.   For the pardons gain'd
Seem'd always difficult to be obtain'd,
As if they rather came through intercession
Than from the purpose of his own remission
And lenitie (which commonly incites
A boldeness in disorder'd appetites
To more offence) thus wisely managèd,
Offensive minds were more discouragèd
By mercie than by justice.   For when they
That stood to die by some unlook'd for way
Were pardon'd, when they did despair to live,
T' observing soldiers instantly did give
Themselves persuasion that undoubtedly
The next offender should be sure to die :
And that opinion like a Centinell
Held watch upon their actions—did repel
Th' extravagant emptions of offence—
Enlarg'd the scope of care and diligence,
And did not onely hold a regular
And orderly obedience to the warre

But like-wise did as happily prevent
The just necessitie of punishment
On many lives, which, under milder course,
Presumption would incur, and law,—of force
To cut off ways to dangerous consequence,—
Must execute. Thus, that which in the sense
Of vulgar apprehension seem'd to bee
A disposition unto crueltie,
Appear'd a worke that wisedome did project
With purpose to a contrarie effect.
That which malignant censure would suggest
To be a humour cruellie express'd
That did men's lives regardlessly deprive,
Was of men's lives the best preservative
But, to disproove that idle imputation
That made it seeme a vitious inclination
Inherent with his nature, and augment
The force of his true honour's argument,—
Offences done against his owne estate
(Which alwayes doth more strongly aggravate
The weight of injurie to private sense
Than public apprehension of offence
And stirres men's passions more) have oftentimes

Subduc'd the malefactors for those crimes
Into the hands of justice, where he might
With approbation and consent of right
Have satisfied that nature to the full,
As well in punishments that justly pull
On death, as other grievous penalties.
And yet his hurt that from those faults did rise
And nearly touch'd him, never did incense
Or moove his mind (since with no reference
They did engage him to the publique cause).
To prosecute the rigour of the lawes
But held himself sufficiently content
To learne by one, another to prevent.
Nor need I from his martial scope digress
T' approve that by his morall cariges
Since, if we doe proceede to note his course,
We shall observe, where mildness was of force
To propagate the armies service more
Than stern-ness,—with conformitie he bore
Himselfe.   As in the exercise of armes
(Where terrour alwaies generally harmes
And dulles the apprehension and conceipt)
Hee hated roughness, violence and heate,

And with a most un-weari'd patientness
Would labour to insinuate and impresse
His demonstrations.   Hence it might appeare
He had a mind so temperatelie cleare
And free from passion, that he could applie
His methode to his subjects propertie ;
And both approve that his severitie
Was dedicated to utilitie.
Wherein his nature did itself expresse
Adapted unto publique bus'neses
That had the strength of patience to despise
The bitter censures of malignancies
In managements so subject to construction ;
And fixe himselfe upon the right conduction
Of his affaires, to publique use design'd
Nor giv'n nor forc'd to any other end.
He was not of that soft and servile mould
That all impressions takes and none doth hold
But his owne reason in himself did raigne
What she inspir'd he firmly did retaine.
He could not flatter greatness : Zanie* humours

* The verb *Zany,* to mimic or imitate, is not uncommon in the
Elizabethan writers. Cf. Beaumont and Fletcher's *Queen of Corinth.*
" All excellence
In other madams does but *Zanie* hers ;"

Or be obsequious t' aswage the tumours
That in corrupted minds did rise and swell
Against him.   But did residently dwell
Upon the purpose of a true intent
In whose succeses he was confident.
And as his word was all his deeds were so
"—— *Veritate non obsequio.*"

Thus did his armie in obedience stand
Under the count'nance of a brave command
Which, from the force his wisdom did applie
Receiv'd more strength than from 's authoritie
And as the disposition of the mind
Was by his governement well disciplin'd
So was the bodie by his exercise
Practic'd and perfect in th' activities
And postures, on the which consist the right
Wayes of agilitie and skill to fight
In arms and armies ; where his hand did show
As much as reason and experience know

and in *Lovelace :*

> " As I have seen an arrogant baboon
> With a small piece of glass zany the moon."

Tourneur uses it in the sense of flatter or be subservient to.

How they should marshall them ; how to compose
Divide, transpose, convert, open or close
Partes, bodies, figures, aspects, distances
In quarter, march, attempts, resistances,
According as the ground's capacity
Or the condition of an enemy
Requireth or admits the fittest course
Of forme or change ; with order speede and force
And best assurance from defensive art.
To'th most advantage in th' offensive part
And all those other partes, whereof consist
The gen'rall worth of such a martialist
In him united their habilities
And made him compleate.   All his industries
(As well in actives as contemplatives)
Were such as those whence Providence derives
Apt instruments to stand in present stead
According to th' occasion offerèd
Which either on the principall dessigne
Or some adherent int'rests that entwine
And sway the principall, may fasten on
An answerable disposition
And so work way to prosperous events

As well in unexpected accidents
As things projected and premeditate.

   In Councell he was of so temperate
And free a mind, that Reason in his soul
Like an imperiall presence did controule
And silence all those passions that have force
To interrupt the passage of discourse,
While to the cleare and uneclipsèd eye
Of his strong intellectuall faculty
His well-informèd knowledge did present
The state and nature of the argument;
The parts : th' entire ; and every circumstance
That was contingent, or had reference
Materiall to the thing consulted on.
Which when his free discourse had pass'd upon,
His judgment in conclusion did lay ope
The waies, the meanes, the reasons, and the scope.
What, how, whereby and *when,* and *where* to do
And every due respect annex'd unto
With such demonstrative and pregnant force
That practise without speculative discourse,
Nor speculation without practise tried,
Nor both without great prudence amplified

To know their uses and apply them well,
To his advise could make a parallel.

Nor did his knowledge and experience stand
Upon that onely limit of command
That marshalleth an army fit to fight,
But had as perfect and profound a sight
Into the judgment how it should be led
And with the most advantage managed
As well through all the bodie of a war
As in performance of particular
Dependent services : as they may note
Who have perused how his pen did quote
The margent of our Ages great designs
With his observing and judicious lines.*
And in those objects of the judgement's eie,
As if he kept a key of mysterie,
His understanding had so deepe a sight

---

* This doubtless refers to the Commentaries of Sir Francis Vere, which Tourneur must have seen in MS., as they were not published till they came into the hands of Dr. William Dellingham, who gave them to the world in 1657. It was, however, well known at the time that Vere had written them, and transcripts had been taken of them by his friends : two, for instance are recorded by Dellingham himself, one in the possession of the Earl of Westmoreland, the other in the hands of Lord Fairfax.

That in dessignes which were without the light
Of practise or example he hath found
Oft times a way which, when he did propound,
Was of so difficult and high a straine
That e'en experienc'd sense could hardl' attain
To find it probable or fit, unlesse
Approved by demonstration and success.
Yet of true judgement constant in pursuit
When action did his counsaile execute
The progress and event, subscrib'd in act
His way for largest use was most exact.
Nor was his judgement only so mature
In purposes whose distance could endure
Deliberate advise, but did expresse
Itself as fully ripe with readiness
And order, where the case would not admit
The action any time to studie it,
And had so present a conceipt that did
Attend occasion as it offered,
That when the thunder of a hotte alarme
Hath call'd him sodainly from sleepe to arme
Upon the instant of his waking hee
Did with such life and quicke dexteritie

His troupes direct, the service execute,—
As practis'd printers sette and distribute
Their letters,—and more perfectly effected,
For what he did was not to be corrected ;
And as his counsailes shew'd his judgment's merit
So did his deedes as infinite a spirit.
In action both contracted did embrace,
What are perform'd,—was to the other's grace.
There wisedome did his fortitude direct
And fortitude his wisedome did protect.
For in the heart of active services
Where sodaine dangers with a fierce access
Have made surprise upon him, unremov'd
His judgment stood and there was most approv'd.
His understanding's greatness did appeare
In perturbations, least disturb'd, most cleare,
And then gave amplest witness of her worth ;
All the directions he deliver'd forth
Were then most orderly assur'd and sound.
The sense of terrour never could confound
His judgement.   Reason did such freedom find
Within the generous greatness of his mind,
And was so guarded by his fortitude

From ev'ry violence that would intrude,
Which, in such dangers, doth precisely trie
The true and native magnanimitie.
For nothing doth the judgement more torment
With rude confusion and astonishment
Than feare,* which by contraction of the hart
Doth force the powers of soul from ev'ry part
Out of their proper seats and offices
Into a narrow lymitt, where the presse
And undistinguish'd crowde of faculties
Doth interrupt the passage of advice.
Hence not improperly the word might rise
That terms them little minds which cowardize
Possesseth ; where, when fear of death doth start
The spirits and makes them fly unto the heart
They want that competent requirèd space
For ev'ry power in a distinguish'd place
To work in order.   Consequently thence
It may be taken in as apt a sence
Courage is termèd greatness of the mind
Where reason with her faculties doth find

* This is possibly borrowed from Lucretius' explanation of the
causes of the emotions. Cf. De Rer. Nat., particularly II. 962,
seqq.

Sufficient roome wherein she may dilate
These sev'ral properties with ordinate
Distinction (when invasive terrours rise
Upon th' exterior senses to surprise
These passages) by making good their grounds
Unto the largeness of their proper bounds.
Yet may we not deservedly repute
That nature worthy this great attribute
Where boundless choler doth predominate,—
For that extention's rather vast than great
And by extreamnès in another kind
As dangerously disturbes the powers of mind
As Fear* contrudes, so Choler doth disperse.
But Fortitude, nor violently fierce
Nor coldly dull, as prudence doth require
Holds them distinguish'd, mutuall, and entire.
For that which is a vertue will admit
All vertue free societie with it.
And this was that true valour which the spirit
Of this heroique worthy did inherit.
Now if malignant censure quarrels it
And says† it was a habite he did get
By custom with such danger rather than

* *Lat.* Contrudere.   † *Orig.* say.

The native vertue of a valiant man
Let Envie please to turn her clearer eye
On his beginnings : they will satisfie
Or prove her false. For when he first bore armes
Among the first that press'd to front alarmes
His sword thrust foremost, and his chief desire
From the beginning labour'd to aspire
Through enterprise and danger. When the face
Of bloodie-handed war in it's owne place
Did first encounter him, and did appeare
In shapes of terrour to impresse a feare
He met it smiling, and did make it yield
That he brought courage with him to the field.
And when but in a private ranque he served
That vertue made him publiquely observ'd,
And was th' effectuall cause that did advance
His fortunes to a higher countenance.
The first examples of his worth in act
Were like to that where valour did attract
Th' impartial eye of valiant Williams,* and

---

* Roger Williams, a famous general at that time, was born at
Penrose, in Monmouthshire, and was educated at Oxford. After
quitting the University, he became a volunteer in the army of the
Duke of Alva. He was knighted, according to Anthony Wood, in
1586, doubtless for his services under Norris in Friesland. Amid

In honour of him published with his hand
In a discourse now extant,* then put forth
Where he to this† effect, reports his worth
" Brave Vere was by his scarlet cassock known
Who at th' assaults both of the fort and towne
Stood alwies in the head of th' armèd men,
Where having twice been hurt and wounded when
Myself (with other of his friends' desire)
Requested him that then he would retire
His answer was, that *he had rather die*
Ten times upon a breach than once to lie

---

many courageous exploits in the Low Countries, he assisted, 1591, in
the siege of Dieppe. He died in London, 1595. He is the author
of " A Discourse of the Discipline of the Spaniards," " A brief
Discourse of War, with his opinion concerning some parts of the
Martial Discipline, 1590," and of a small quarto of 133 pages, entitled " The Actions of the Low Countries," which is in point of
style bald and uncouth, in point of matter interesting and valuable.
His " Briefe Discourse " is a manly, sensible little work, stamped
with the mark of a bold, shrewd, observant intellect.

* The discourse now extant is " The Briefe Discourse of Warre,"
and the passage versified by Tourneur is to be found in page 58, and
runs thus : " Also Sir Francis Vere, marked for his red mandilion,
who stood alwaies in the head of the armed men at the assaults of the
Fort and Toune ; being twice hurt, I and other his friends requested
him to retire, he answered he had rather be kild ten times at a
breach, than once in a house," &c.

† *Orig.* his.

Under the hand of death within a house," &c.
Thus at the first his understanding showes
Itself and no occasion doth admit
That might give witness of his worth to it.
And, as his courage then was true to th' wayes
Through which hee did 's deserved fortunes raise
To his particular and private good ;
So for the publique service when he stood
It ever was so faithful to the lawes
Of that integritie he ought* the cause
He serv'd, that when occasion did present
His observation with some accident
Within the enemie, that did invite
The side he served in to attempt a fight,
With promise of good service to the state,—
Though dangers might make it infortunate
To his particular, and did object
Then terrours to disanimate th' effect,—
And though the presence of superiour place
Did show no disposition to embrace
The enterprise—when nothing did enforce
His courage but his voluntary course,

* The old preterite.

If promise of good service did invite,
Through dangers he expos'd himself to fight
Against all difficulties that withstood
And wonne his honour with his losse of blood.
And what his sword could not directly hit
He circumvented by the power of wit
Using that license only which in warre;
Hath just allowance though irregular,
Where he shew'd all wherein wit can assist
The workings of a stratagematist—
Without conducting them to their successe
Through any passage of perfidiousness.
And th' undertakings of his industrie
Were carried with such dext'rous secrecie
That while the breath of his divulg'd pretence,
Suited with fit ostentiall instruments,
Transported expectation to that face
And made him look'd for in another place
His expedition ere it was suspected
Set forth, arriv'd, attempted and effected,
And where his purposes required no name
His actions ever march'd before their fame

And (for a close) to crowne his worth, bless'd Fate

Did render all his actions fortunate
Witness the best performances of war
Whereby th' united Netherlanders are
Entirely of their own provinces possess'd
With advantageous footing on the rest.
'Mongst which atchieuements* Niewport and Os-
    tend,†
Those famous services, doe comprehend
Large interest in the deserts, whereby
They have attained to that prosperitie

* This battle, in which Vere greatly distinguished himself, and of
which he gives a minute account in his "Commentaries," was fought
in 1600.

† Ostend.   This was perhaps the most brilliant of all Vere's
achievements.

Ostend was in 1601 besieged by the Archduke Albert, and Vere,
who had been appointed general of the army of the States about
Ostend, entered the city 11th of July, 1601, to defend it.   With a
mere handful of men, 1600 or 1700, he resolutely and triumphantly
resisted the whole force of the Spanish army, which numbered about
12,000, for eight months.   On August 14th he was severely wounded
by the bursting of a cannon, and that obliged him to retire for a
while into Zealand.   On his return to Ostend he repulsed a sharp
attack made by the Spaniards on the night of December 4th, and
crowned his magnificent services by repelling with only 1200 en-
feebled men the grand assault made by the enemy, 10,000 strong, on
January 7th, 1602, and compelled them to raise the siege.

And of those actions, they themselves confesse
He was an instrument to the successe
Elected by Heav'n's high omnipotence
To manifest his gracious providence
In favour of their cause.   Nor did he less
In any of his other services,
And when the glory of the war did cease
Retir'd with honour—and expir'd in peace.
Leaving his deathlesse memory and fame
To be an honour to that noble name
And familie from whom he had descent
Which by his lustre's made more eminent—.
And now, Great Britain, though thou dost possess
The sov'raigne joy of peace and happiness
And feelst no reason why thou should'st disperse
Or spend a teare upon a souldier's hearse
Yet for the sake e'en of thy blessèd peace
Thou maist lament this worthy man's decease.
For war's a subject that may comprehend
The greatest wisedome nature can extend
Unto, to manage it, whose noblest wayes
Prov'd him a Worthy, Heroe of his days.

His praise may justly then extend thus farre,
Hee was a man fit both for peace and warre
Whose monument while Historie doth last
Shall never be forgotten or defac'd.

THREE ELEGIES

on

The most lamented Death

of

PRINCE HENRIE.

The First ⎱
The Second ⎬ WRITTEN BY ⎰ *Cyril Tourneur.*
The Third ⎰ ⎱ *John Webster.*
                         Tho. Heywood.

LONDON:
Printed for *William Welbie.*
1613

A

GRIEFE

On the Death

Of PRINCE HENRIE,

Expressed in a Broken
Elegie, according to the nature of
such a Sorrow,

By *Cyril Tovrnevr.*

LONDON:
Printed for *William Welbie.*
1613

TO MY NOBLE
MAISTER MR. GEORGE CARIE.

SIR ; It was a season for Elegies of this kind when I
wrote this, before His funeralls.   I had no purpose
(then) to have it published.   Importunity hath since
drawne it from me.   But my first intent of dedication is
not altered.   It cannot ; unless I could change myself.
And (besides the subscription of my duety to you) you
deserve to be acknowledged in this argument among His
true mourners, for you honouerd him much and faithfully.
For which, no lesse than for any other part of your
generous disposition, I am and will bee

Your servant,

CYRIL TOVRNEVR.

TO THE READER.

I cannot blame thee if thou readst not right

Or understandst not, for I know thy sight

With weeping is imperfect, if not blind,

And sorrow does almost distract thy mind.

C. T.

A GRIEFE ON

THE DEATH OF
PRINCE HENRIE, EXPRES-
SED IN A BROKEN ELEGIE, ACCORDING
TO THE NATURE OF SUCH A
SORROW.

OOD Vertue wipe thine eyes.   Look up and
    see !
         And wonder to behold it.   Some there be
That weep not ; but are strangely merrie, dance
And revell.   Can the loss of him advance
The heart of any man to such a mirth ?
Can his grave be the womb, from whence the birth
Of Pleasure riseth ?   *Pity them.   Their woe
Distracts 'em and they know not what they doe.*
Yet note 'em better.   Be they wicked men
Their shew of joy is voluntarie then,
For now the President of virtue's dead,
Vice hopes to get her courses licencèd

14—2

Dead ! 'Tis above my knowledge how we live

To speak it.   Is there any faith to give

The promises of health or remedy ?

Or any meane to be preservèd by,

When* temperance and exercise of breath

Those best physicians could not keep from death

The strength of Nature ?   Was Hee temperate?   Whence

Then came hee subject to the violence

Of sicknesse ?   Rather was He not inclin'd

To pleasures ?   Infinitely : still His mind

Was on them infinitely ; for His love

No objects had, but those which were above

The causes of vexation, such, as done,

Repented not the pleasures they begun,

But made them endless : Nothing had the might

To diseffect his actions of delight ;

* With Tourneur's Poetry may be compared Birch's prose, who says " Life of Henry, Prince of Wales," p. 385, 386.

" His temperance, except in the article of fruit, was as eminent as his abhorrence of vanity and ostentation . . . . . His exercises were of the most manly kind. `He used almost daily to ride and manage great horses ; often to run at the ring and sometimes at tilt. His other exercises were dancing, leaping, etc. He sometimes walked fast and far, to accustom and enable himself to make long marches."

No, nor his sufferings.   For* although Hee knew
That sickness came from earth to claim her due
And to deprive him of that fortunate
Succession to the greatness of the state
Which Hee was borne to : that did likewise please
And added nothing unto His disease.
Of his contentments heere, that was the best,
Therefore the last, that it might crowne the rest.
But these are not the pleasures that decay†
The body.   How hath death then found a way
To one so able?   Hee was yong and strong,
Unguiltie of all disorder that could wrong
His constitution.   Doe no longer hide
It : t'was to us a plague whereof Hee died

---

* Cf. again Birch.

"For pleasures in general, he used them only as it were in passage, without seeming to desire them, or at least to have any inclination to indulge them.   He never desired to live long, often saying that it was to small purpose for a brave, gallant man, when the prime of his days were past, to live till he were full of diseases."

† For this not uncommon meaning of the neuter verb, cf. Shakspeare.

"Twelfth Night," i. 5.—"Infirmity that decays the wise doth ever make better the fool.   And even so late as Addison.   "It is so ordered that almost everything that corrupts the soul decays the body."— "Guardian," No. 120.

A plague by much more common to us then
The last great sicknesse many more the men
Who suffer in it.*   That which now is gone
Was but the figure of a greater One
To follow.   Since the first that e'er was borne
A fuller number was not known to mourne.
For all the old men of the kingdomes weepe
Since He that promis'd by His strength to keepe
Their children free from others violence
And, by example, from their own offence,
Is taken from 'em.   And they would have died
When he did, but for tarrying to provide
A second care for that they would have left
To Him, of whose protection th' are bereft.
If we doe well consider their just woes
We must include our yong men too in those,
And grieve for ever.   For our old men's teares
Are rather for the time to come than theirs.
If they that shall not live to suffer much
Under this cause of sorrow, utter such

---

* See Birch's "Life of Henry Prince of Wales," p. 333, and
Chapman's "Epicedium," with his note, and cf. Cornwallis' "Account of the Life and Death of Henry," etc.

A passion for it : more it does belong
To us that now are growing to it : yong
As if our generation had intent
We should be borne to feele the punishment.
Now let us willingly give griefe regard
Lest we be forc'd to do it afterward
By Heav'ns just anger. Stay a little. Why
Should yong men thinke the old shall sooner die ?
His youth's great broken promise wee complaine,
Yet none was greater. And are ours less vaine ?
Mistake not. As humanity now goes
Hee liv'd a man as long as any does.
For* onelie in those minutes that wee give
To virtue wee are trulie said to live
Men, and no longer. If we reckon then
His good houres with the good of other men,
His time's whole added numbers will arise
To his that tells our fourscore ere he dies.
To proove this, looke as low as e'er you can
And hear the words of the dejected man
The souldier speaks them. *Honour ! Now I see*

---

* A well-known Stoic maxim on which Seneca, Epist. 15, and elsewhere, is fond of preaching his rambling sermons.

There is no hope that any age will be
So good and noble as the ancient were,
None so heroic ever shall appear.
For if that fate which cannot be withstood
Had not decreed there should be none so good
Shee would not have neglected such a worth
As His was, to have brought that great worke forth.
And having purpos'd it should never be,
And hearing everywhere by Fame, that he
Was making one, she kill'd him. Mark his eye
Hee weepes. He weeps that can more easilie
Weepe bloud than water. Then I wonder how
Or he or anye other souldier now
Can hold his sword unbroken, since * Hee was
That gave them count'nance. That's the cause, alas,
They doe not breake them, and a just excuse
They wear them now, to keep them from abuse.
For that great favour now has made an end
That their despis'd conditions did defend.
Artes too are so discourag'd by their harmes
In losse of him who lov'd both them and armes

---

　* An awkward English application of the common Latin euphe-
mism for dying.

That they would all leave studie and decline
From learning, if those naturall and divine
Persuading contemplations did not leade
The one to Heaven, the other to the Dead.
Between whose parts they have divided his
And promise so to bring them where Hee is,
But I would have their studies never die
For preservation of his memorie.
How can *that* perish? That will ever keepe
Because th' impression of it is so deepe.
When any painter to the life that saw
His presence fullie, takes in hand to draw
An Alexander or a Cæsar, his best
Imaginations will bee so possess'd
With His remembrance that as hee does limme
Hee'l make that worthie's picture like to him,
And then t'will be a piece of such a grace
For height and sweetness, as that only face
Will make another painter, that ne'er knew
Him living, follow as the other drew.
How great a character deserves Hee then
Whose memorie shall but expire with men!
When a Divine or Poet sets downeright

What other Princes should bee, He shall unite
What this was.   That's His character which beares
My sorrow inward, to go forth in teares ;
Yet some of joy too, mix'd with those of greefe
That flow from apprehension of releefe.
I see his spirit turn'd into a starre
Whose influence makes that His own virtues are
Succeeded justlie, otherwise the worst,
As at His funerall, should proceede the first.
His native goodness follows in his roome
Else good men would be buried in His tombe.

    O ! suffer this to be a faithfull verse
    To live for ever, weeping o'er his herse.

                        CYRIL TOURNEUR.

ON THE REPRESEN-
TATION OF THE
PRINCE AT HIS FUNERALLS.

E that the life of this face ever saw,
The mildness in it noting and the awe,
Will judge that peace did either in her love
So soone advance him to her state above,
Or else, in feare that He would warre preferre,
Concluded with Him he should live with her.
To both His aptnesse fluently appeares
In ev'rie souldier's grief and schollar's teares.

C. T.

END OF VOL. I.